Little Hearts Books

Two Thousand Kisses a Day
Gentle Parenting Through the
Ages and Stages

Children's book and parenting author, L.R.Knost, is an
independent child development researcher and founder and
director of the advocacy and consulting group, Little
Hearts/Gentle Parenting Resources, as well as a monthly
contributor to *The Natural Parent Magazine*. She is also a
babywearing, breastfeeding, co-sleeping, homeschooling mother
of six. Her children are a twenty-five-year-old Pastor and
married father of two; a twenty-three-year-old married Family
Therapist working on an advanced degree; an eighteen-year-old
university pre-med student on scholarship; thirteen- and six-
year-old sweet, funny, socially active, homeschooled girls; and
an adorable twenty-five-month-old nursling. Other works by
L.R.Knost include the *Wisdom For Little Hearts* series and the
soon-to-be-released *Grumpykins* series of children's picture
books which are humorous and engaging tools for parents,
teachers, and caregivers to use in implementing gentle parenting
techniques in their homes and schools.

*Note: Information contained in this book is for educational
purposes only and should not be construed as medical advice.

Two Thousand Kisses a Day
Gentle Parenting Through the Ages and Stages

L.R.Knost

A Little Hearts Handbook
Little Hearts Books, LLC. ▪ U.S.A.

Photography credit: Melissa Lynsay Photography

Dedicated to my six little and not-so-little blessings…

I am your midnight hug

I am your midnight hug ~ Whether you're a teething baby or a scared toddler or a broken-hearted teen, I'll be there day or night.

I am your helping hand ~ When you need help climbing up the big slide or building the science project or bringing your own baby into the world, you can count on me.

I am your best friend ~ Whether you're happy or sad, good or bad, joyful or mad, I'll share your joys and sorrows, encourage and guide you, and care enough to always tell you the truth.

I am your example ~ I'll respect you so you learn to respect, listen so you'll learn to listen, forgive so you'll learn to forgive, show compassion so you'll learn to be kind, and be honest so you'll learn to tell the truth.

I am your safe place ~ When you fail, when you fall, when you're hurting, come to me, and I'll be here with open arms.

I am your pep squad ~ When you try, I'll root you on. When you succeed, I'll cheer 'til I'm hoarse. When you fail, I'll hug you close and whisper, "One more time."

I am your protector ~ Whether you're a frightened toddler or a bullied teen, I'm in your corner with gloves on, ready to help you take on the world.

I am your confidant ~ Whether you're proud of yourself and need to toot your own horn or ashamed and need to confess your mistakes, I'm here to listen and understand.

I am your parent, but I'm not perfect ~ When I do something wrong, I'll admit it. When I'm hurting, I'll let you help. When I'm struggling, I won't pretend everything is okay. I'll be real so we can have a real relationship.

As long as I'm alive, you'll always have arms ready to hug you, ears ready to listen to you, and a heart that will never stop loving you.

~ Mom

Table of Contents

Middle Childhood: Becoming Their Own Person

Gentle Parenting: Teens and Beyond

Conclusion: Setting Yourself Up For Success

References

~ Introduction ~

Chapter 1

*Two Thousand Kisses a Day to
Two Thousand Connection Points a Day*

From kicking and rolling and stretching to being lulled to sleep by the rhythmic cadence of a mama's heartbeat, little ones spend the first months of their existence wrapped in a warm, dark, gently swaying cocoon, a life-giving embrace, the ultimate hug, readying themselves for their grand entrance to the world.

Then, in those first moments of life beyond the womb, when the muffled sounds of the outside world become clear and the muted lights become glaringly bright, a warm breast with the sweet scent of life-sustaining milk and the soothing sound of a familiar heartbeat welcome the little one to the comfort and safety of a mama's arms.

In the days, weeks, and months that follow, little fingers and toes are counted and kissed again and again and again. Soft cheeks are snuzzled, and a fuzzy little head is nuzzled, and two thousand kisses a day seems a reasonable number to a mama's heart overflowing with tenderness for this tiny new member of the family.

Then comes the rolling and sitting and crawling and walking, and soon the two thousand kisses a day dwindle to brief morning cuddles before a toddler is off to explore the world, healing kisses on boo-boos, and goodnight snuggles with a bedtime book.

Time passes and little ones grow in independence, getting up and dressed and ready on their own, grabbing their own bandage for a scrape, and reading themselves to sleep. Gone are the snuzzles and nuzzles of infancy, and the two thousand kisses a day are simply sweet memories.

Growing independence, though, doesn't have to mean growing separation. Humans were created to be relational beings. We may outgrow our dependency, but we never outgrow the need for community, interaction, appreciation, reassurance, and support.

Infants, children, and adults alike all share this life-long need for connection. Over time that need will also be met through friendships, business engagements, social interactions, and the like; but family relationships are the steady and sure bedrock of secure connection and belonging that ground us and assure us that our needs will not go unmet even in the darkest of times.

Meeting that human need for secure connection is what gentle parenting is all about. Unfortunately, gentle, attachment-style parenting is often misconstrued to be simply about breastfeeding, babywearing, and co-sleeping. But, while those are possible choices for creating a secure parent/child connection in the early years, they are just a small sampling of the relationship-building and maintaining choices that parents can make throughout their children's lives.

As little ones outgrow the 'two thousand kisses a day' stage, parents can begin consciously creating 'two thousand connection points a day' to replace those tender expressions of love with age-appropriate expressions of appreciation and approval, love and support.

From responding empathetically to a preschooler's whine, to paying attention to a seven-year-old when they tell their endless stories, to listening 'between the lines' to the angst of a teen, maintaining a secure parent/child connection beyond infancy is simply about meeting emotional needs consistently, intentionally, and relationally.

Creating two thousand connection points a day isn't about quality time, and it isn't even about the quantity of time spent with our children. It is, instead, about being there in the small moments, the moments that matter to our children, and consciously meeting with them right where they are. It is about...

- Simply smiling and letting our eyes light up with welcome when our children walk in the room

- Maintaining eye contact when our children talk to us instead of letting our eyes constantly stray back to our laptops or cell phones or televisions

- Voicing our sincere appreciation for their latest 'masterpiece,' victory, or achievement

- Expressing our affection physically in whatever way our children are comfortable with, whether it's a dog-pile-on-daddy wrestling match, a knuckle pound, or a hug

- Giving our children our undivided, wholehearted attention when they share their latest treasure or sing a never-ending song they make up as they go or just want to sit and be close for awhile

- Listening to what our children need to say without them feeling the threat of repercussion

- Inferring what they aren't able to express verbally

- Inviting our children into our daily lives, whether we are discussing politics or cooking dinner or fixing the car

- Allowing our children to express their emotions, even when those emotions aren't pretty

- Validating their anger, hurt, frustration, or embarrassment instead of minimizing or dismissing their feelings

- Helping them to process those emotions by listening to them and reflecting back what we hear

- Guiding them toward the understanding of their own feelings and empathetically equipping them with coping mechanisms for the future

- Sharing our own hurts, disappointments, and mistakes in age-appropriate terms so they'll know it's okay to be human

- Honoring our children's intense need to avoid embarrassment by offering guidance privately and respectfully, even if their behavior issue is public and/or disrespectful

- Sharing their interests even if the life-cycle of a snail wouldn't be our first choice of dinner conversation

- Offering choices so they can grow in independence and confidence

- Supporting them even when their choices lead to disappointment or failure

- Being gently and kindly and completely honest about our own disappointment or hurt when their behavior negatively affects us, so they'll know they can trust us to be truthful, even in the hard things

- Helping them whenever and wherever they express a need for assistance so they'll know they never have to cope with life alone

These connection points are about maintaining and enriching a strong parent/child relationship through all of the ages and stages of childhood so that, through a foundation of trust and mutual respect, parenting takes the form of guiding instead of punishing, encouraging natural growth instead of forcing premature independence, and creating a strong, intimate, interwoven family fabric that will stand the test of time.

We must always keep in mind, though, that gentle parenting is a journey, not a destination. From the first awareness that a new life is growing, through infancy, toddlerhood, the preschool years, middle childhood, the teen years, and on into young adulthood, we are learning to be parents in the boots-on-the-ground, learn-as-we-go school of parenthood. No matter how prepared we are, there will always be unexpected challenges as surely as there will be unexpected joys, and we will always need to be willing to stretch and grow and learn.

So, let's get started on the journey to gentle parenting…

Chapter 2

Surviving the First Three Months with a Newborn

So, your precious baby has finally arrived. After a perfect pregnancy and blissful labor and delivery, you've come home (in your pre-pregnancy clothes, of course) with your beautiful baby, ready to start life as the perfect parent of a perfect child.

Yeah, *right*! Actually, after a pregnancy in which you threw up more times than you can count and yet still managed to gain an embarrassing amount of weight, and where your feet swelled to unrecognizable lumps at the bottom of your legs, you finally suffered through a hideously long, painful labor and delivery only to arrive home (in your largest maternity outfit which barely fit!) with a screaming, vomiting, miniature human being who can't tell you why he's upset and who poops what can best be described as TAR! What are you going to do now?!?

First, call your mommy! No, really, if you have a mom or grandmother or aunt or good friend who has any experience with babies, ask for help. As long as there have been babies being born, there have been women gathering around to help new mamas through those first intense weeks with a newborn. Experienced helpers can make all the difference in how well you survive the sleepless nights, crazy hormones, and vast uncertainties that come with being a new parent.

Beware, though, the experienced helpers who are a bit *too* helpful and try to push you out of the way even to the extent of trying to guilt you into leaving your baby behind to go on a walk or a date-night 'for the good of your marriage.' In the first place, having to leave your baby behind to preserve your marriage isn't a great precedent to set with your husband. You two are in this together and setting a precedent of *family* first is a good idea! And secondly, the whole point of having help is not only for you to recover, but also so you can become experienced yourself in taking care of your baby.

Second, while accepting help is vital, make sure that everyone knows that this baby is *your* baby and *you* will decide what is best for you and your child. Listen to all the advice, then take what makes sense to you and ignore the rest. Let your helpers do the housework and the cooking and the errands while you take care of and get to know the new little addition to your family. If your instincts tell you to hold your baby, even while she sleeps, then hold your baby even while she sleeps. If your instincts tell you to nurse your crying baby even though you just nursed fifteen minutes ago, then nurse your baby. God gave you those instincts for a reason, so don't ignore them!

Third, you've most likely already heard the 'sleep when your baby is sleeping' advice. Listen to that advice. Short little naps may not seem all that helpful in theory, but they can be life-savers when getting used to the rigors of new parenthood. And keep reminding yourself that it will get better because it will!

Fourth, whether you've chosen to breastfeed or bottle-feed, expect your little one to eat erratically right at first. Remember, babies' nutritional needs were met with a constancy and lack of effort in utero that can't be fully replicated outside of the womb. Their tummies are only about the size of a walnut in the first days, so they can't eat enough at a feeding to last them more than two or three hours at most, and often far less. Also, if you're breastfeeding it's common to worry that your baby isn't getting enough milk, but if you keep in mind how tiny their little tummies are you'll realize that it doesn't take much to fill them up. Things to consider with breastfeeding are getting a good latch and establishing your supply, among others, and it's often helpful to consult a lactation specialist for guidance. There are excellent resources available in most communities through your local hospital or La Leche League as well as online resources such as Kellymom.com and Best for Babes.

Fifth, while bathing your baby may be fun, it really isn't necessary in the first weeks and might be rather traumatic for your little one. 'Topping and tailing' is a term that means taking a warm, wet cloth (no soap) and gently washing their eyes (inner corner to outer corner to avoid infection), face, ears, head, and neck, and then washing their bottom, being careful to clean out all the little cracks and crevices. Follow that with cord care (gently cleaning the cord area with a cotton swab) and you're done!

Sixth, birth is a huge transition for a baby. From a warm, dark, weightless environment where all their needs are met, sounds are muffled, and mama's heartbeat lulls them to sleep, they are abruptly ejected into a cold, loud, bright world where they experience hunger and discomfort and loneliness and fear for the first time. You can help your little one cope by easing the transition. Keeping the lights a bit dimmer and the sounds a bit more muted right at first is helpful in welcoming your baby to your world. Also, it's helpful to wear your baby in those first transitional weeks and often far longer when you discover how convenient it is. Babywearing is a term that refers to using a baby carrier, wrap, or sling to keep your baby close to you where he can hear your heartbeat and feel your warmth and closeness in an approximation of your womb. All of these things will help to reduce your baby's stress as he acclimates to his new environment, and a less stressed baby tends to result in a less stressed mommy!

Seventh, there is a big divide in parenting circles between the 'bed-sharers' and the 'crib-sleepers' so be aware that whichever choice you make will probably be challenged by more than one of your friends or relatives. Bottom line, whatever sleeping arrangement you choose, be sure to follow safe sleeping guidelines (more on this in the next chapter), and then follow your instincts. If you choose to put your little one in a crib or bassinet, though, do yourself a favor and put it next to your bed to reduce your travel time in the middle of the night. You'll thank me, I promise!

Eighth, your baby is completely and totally helpless in every way. Her main mode of communication is crying. Medical experts agree that it isn't possible to spoil a newborn[1] and you are just at the beginning stages of building a trust relationship, so respond promptly to your little one's cries! Your immediate response to your baby's needs will help her begin to learn that she can count on you when she needs you and that she doesn't have to fight for your attention. Babies left to cry-it-out often do sleep through the night sooner than babies whose needs are responded to because they have learned to give up on having their needs met. But that supposed gain of sleeping through the night is accomplished through a loss of trust, and the long-term consequences of a child giving up on her parents simply aren't worth it.

Ninth, baby yourself! Whether you've had a vaginal birth or a c-section, your body has been through the wringer; your hormones are all over the place; and your lack of sleep is not helping matters. Have someone make you a 'survival basket' (or make one for yourself before your baby arrives) with water bottles, granola bars, minty sugar-free gum, hand sanitizer, diapers, baby wipes, burp rags, and, most importantly, chocolate! The basket should be small and light enough for you to take from room to room with you while carrying your baby. Also, have someone make a comfy area in your living room for you to nurse (with your survival basket within reach!) and a changing area so you don't have to go back and forth to the bedroom or nursery throughout the day. Take showers when you can. Accept casseroles and other offerings of meals from friends and church members and co-workers. If you don't have help for the housework, just do the bare minimum so you can rest and recover and focus on getting to know your precious new baby.

Tenth, baby your marriage! This is a huge, huge, huge transition for you and your husband, so apologize to each other in advance for any temper tantrums, thoughtless words, or unmet needs that might (will!) occur in the foreseeable future. You are going from 'the two of us' to 'we three' and just as with anything else, change isn't easy. Husbands, sorry, but it's not about you right now, period. Yes, you have your own issues to deal with in becoming a parent for the first time, but you need to put that aside for the first weeks and concentrate on your wife and child. Your wife isn't just having to deal with becoming a mommy, but her body has been through an incredible transition during the past nine months followed by the trauma of labor and delivery followed by crashing hormones and the trials of learning to breastfeed (or dealing with engorgement issues if choosing to bottle feed) and the exhaustion of dealing with a newborn's erratic sleep patterns. If she's also had a c-section, you can add major abdominal surgery to that list. So, husbands, put your own issues aside and baby your wife and baby for the time being. Wives, a little verbal acknowledgement goes a long way with husbands, so try to muster up enough energy to tell your husband that you appreciate him and understand that he is trying to figure out this new life just like you are, and assure him that eventually you will be you again. (Yes, you will. It just takes time!)

Final thoughts: One of the things that has kept me going through giving birth to six children (and losing several others along the way) is the assurance that 'this too shall pass.' As with all changes in life, it takes time to adjust, but reminding yourself that this 'will pass' and you will adjust and life will go on is very, very helpful. Also, take time to enjoy the little things–the sweet smell of your newborn's tiny head, the soft sounds of his breathing as he sleeps, the sight of your spouse staring into your beautiful baby's eyes–because too soon this time *will* pass and these precious moments will become mere beautiful memories.

Chapter 3

Co-Sleeping Like a Baby

Contrary to the old adage 'sleeping like a baby' and contrary to popular opinion, babies are not biologically designed to sleep through the night. Infants and toddlers are natural night-wakers, which has been shown to be protective against the devastation of SIDS (Sudden Infant Death Syndrome).[2] Small children tend to differ not in whether they wake at night or not, but in whether they need help in being soothed back to sleep or not based on their own unique personalities, health issues, environmental factors, etc.

Sleeping patterns are neither a sign of a 'good' baby or a 'bad' baby, just a normal baby. In fact, even adults tend to wake frequently at night, but typically just roll over or adjust their blankets or take a quick trip to the bathroom and then go back to sleep. They just don't often remember any of it in the morning!

In reality, night-waking is simply a biological norm[2] that has been misconstrued as 'problems sleeping' or 'sleep issues' by the demands of our modern, hectic lifestyle. All of those factors, together with the benefit of round-the-clock stimulation of breastmilk production in those first all-important months, makes responding to your baby's nighttime needs as normal and necessary as responding to their daytime needs.

Of course, a need for sustenance is no more worthy of a response than a need for a reassuring cuddle in the dark of the night. I don't know about you, but I, myself, have experienced waking up from a nightmare in the night, shaken and scared, heart pounding, and instinctively reaching out for my husband's hand, knowing that I just needed that warm, human connection for a moment to reassure me, and then I'd be able to go back to sleep.

I've also experienced him not being there at times when he's worked a night shift, and as I lay there, too scared to go back to sleep, I've thought about how it would be to be a helpless baby or small child, scared and alone in the dark, unable to reach out for the comfort of human contact from those I trusted and loved the most. And my heart has broken at the thought of parents who've been misled and intimidated by self-proclaimed parenting 'experts' into sleep-training their precious babies instead of responding to their cries.

Love has many faces, I think we can all agree. Sleep-training parents love their little ones as much as co-sleeping parents, of that I have no doubt. All of us are simply trying to do our best, with the knowledge and experience and belief systems we have, to give our children the best start in life possible.

Responding to your little one's needs swiftly and consistently, though, is the foundation of gentle parenting. That early trust relationship you are building will be the bedrock upon which you will base your connection, communication, and discipline in the years to come.

Co-sleeping is simply the age-old mother's way of meeting a baby's nighttime needs in the most convenient and natural way possible. Co-sleeping can consist of room-sharing, using a side-car attached to your bed, or actually bed-sharing. Room-sharing and using a side-car attachment are no different when it comes to safety measures than putting your baby in their own room as long as you follow the normal safety standards of avoiding crib bumpers and loose sheets, pillows, stuffed animals, blankets, etc. The advantages of room-sharing or using a side-car attachment are, of course, speed and ease in responding to your little one's nighttime needs as well as providing them with the comfort of your presence nearby.

Bed-sharing is the co-sleeping option in which your baby sleeps in bed with you. Many new mamas admit to accidentally falling asleep while nursing their little ones, but that can be dangerous if bed-sharing safety recommendations aren't followed. Those recommendations include the same care in avoiding loose sheets, pillows, stuffed animals, and blankets along with making sure that no one other than a healthy, non-drinking, non-smoking, non-drug using parent is the only one allowed to bed-share with your baby. Before considering co-sleeping, be sure to read all of the safety recommendations from Dr. James J. McKenna, Ph.D. Professor of Biological Anthropology, Director, Mother-Baby Sleep Laboratory, University of Notre Dame.[3]

The advantages of bed-sharing, in addition to the aforementioned speed and ease of response to nighttime needs and the comfort of your presence, are in the increased stimulation of breastmilk production similar to that of kangaroo-care (skin-to-skin) and, as studies have shown, the matching of circadian rhythms (wake/sleep cycles) in mothers and infants which may allow mothers to feel more rested despite the interrupted sleep inherent in caring for a young baby.

Whatever your choice of sleeping arrangements, however, make sure you are able to respond to your baby quickly and safely. Meeting your baby's nighttime needs involves a lot of sacrifice, I know, and it can feel like you'll never get caught up on your sleep again. But the truth is that this season in your baby's life will end before you know it, and the trust relationship you've built will be well worth the sacrifice.

Just as I, an adult mother of six, yearn to have my needs met even when that need is a simple touch to soothe me back to sleep after a nightmare, I want to always try to fill those spaces for my children, day or night. Co-sleeping with our children won't last forever. It's a brief season in a lifetime of ever-changing needs. But it is one face of love that, meets so many needs simply and naturally that I can't imagine life without it.

Here are some ideas for gently weaning your little one into their own sleeping space when the time comes. If you're bed-sharing, start with number one. If you're using a side-car or just room-sharing, start with number two:

1. Place a mattress beside your bed and start out each night there with your little co-sleeper, then you can move up to your bed once your little one is fully asleep. If they wake, be sure to either take them back into your bed with you or join them on the mattress to make the transition as seamless as possible. (You can also start out the night co-sleeping in your bed as usual and then move your little one to a small toddler bed beside your bed once they fall asleep fully if that works better for your space.)

2. When you feel that your little one is comfortable with the new arrangement, move the mattress a bit farther from your bed, either against the wall or at the foot of your bed, and repeat the same process of starting the night with them and welcoming them into your bed or joining them on the mattress if they wake.

3. The next step is to move the mattress into your child's own room and repeat the process, but always be ready to take the process one or two steps backward and start from there if your little one begins to feel uncomfortable.

4. When you feel your child is spending enough time in their room each night to feel comfortable with it, you can try staying with them until they are almost asleep and then telling them you are going to the bathroom or to brush your teeth (make sure you actually do what you say you're going to do!) and will be right back. Come back quickly so they will be reassured that you can still be trusted. If they follow you or get upset, wait and try this step again in a week or two.

5. When they are happy to stay in bed waiting for your return, start letting them spend a bit longer alone. Always tell them what you are going to do, and always do just what you said. Make sure to return when you are done so they know they can trust you and don't need to come get you. If they ever do come get you, simply acknowledge them calmly, "Oh, did you need me already? Okay, let's go back to bed and I'll stay with you as long as you need me," and then sit with them awhile before leaving for a few minutes again or just wait until the next night to try again. As in everything, use your child's comfort level as your guide.

6. Over time, this gradual weaning will generally result in them falling asleep on their own, and you can move on to the stage of books and cuddles and hugs and telling them goodnight, then leaving them with the reassurance that you'll be back to check on them in a bit. Of course, always come back and check like you said you would!

7. Always keep in mind that this is a trust issue. The more that you honor what you say and stay in tune with their needs, the smoother and easier the process will go for both of you.

Chapter 4

Breastfeeding:
The Healthiest Start

Even though mothers' bodies are capable of miraculously growing a human being for nine months and bringing that precious new life into the world, those same life-giving bodies seem to be failing in ever-increasing numbers to provide life-giving nutrition to those precious babies because of issues with low milk supply.

For some, it is certainly just pediatricians using formula-fed babies' growth charts instead of breastfed babies' charts or family and friends who believe that all babies should be chubby and content that lead new mothers to believe they have low supply, but there does appear to be an increasing number of babies legitimately labeled as failure-to-thrive with low milk supply determined to be the cause.

One crucial piece of false information could be to blame for the vast majority of low milk supply issues in the absence of medical issues.

That false information? New mothers are told their babies *should sleep through the night.*

That is one of the most pernicious lies ever foisted on new parents. Babies biologically should *not* sleep through the night. Not only is the deep sleep required to sleep through the night actually a recognized factor in SIDS (Sudden Infant Death Syndrome)[2] as mentioned in the last chapter, but babies who sleep through the night are also not nursing to stimulate breastmilk production, thus their mother's milk may begin to dry up.[4] Clearly, that's not a healthy biological design.

Here is a picture of what this vicious cycle can look like:

Lydia battles the lack of breastfeeding support at the hospital and triumphantly goes home a breastfeeding mother, formula sample tucked securely in a chic little complementary diaperbag provided by the hospital along with stacks of information about how healthy formula is and lots of money-saving formula coupons.

She gets her precious baby home and settles in for her twelve week 'babymoon' before she has to return to work because that's all the time her work allows. She's already nervous about how she's going to handle the return to work, leaving her sweet baby in someone else's care, and trying to pump to maintain her milk supply and provide milk for her baby while she's gone, but she pushes those thoughts aside and suppresses the anxiety as much as she can.

The first few nights are pretty easy because her baby sleeps most of the time, so Lydia is able to get a little rest in between feedings. She reads up on some parenting advice in a couple of popular magazines and discovers that she should be working to schedule her baby's feedings at 3-4 hour intervals. That makes her feel a bit worried because she's just been feeding her baby whenever he seemed hungry, so she gets a notebook out and writes down a schedule.

Over the next couple of weeks, things get a bit more difficult as she walks and bounces and rocks her baby, anxiously watching the clock until she can satisfy her baby's cries and nurse him. Her baby seems to be crying more and more often, though, and, as her stress level increases, she pores over parenting books and magazines trying to find solutions to her baby's distress. Over and over again, she reads that babies need to be on a strict schedule and be trained to self-soothe and sleep through the night.

*Lydia desperately wants to be a good mother, so she braces
herself and stops nursing her baby to sleep, instead laying him
down on his own to fall asleep. She stands outside his door, sobs
shaking her own body as she listens to his screams. But she
confines herself to only occasionally stepping into the room to
pat him gently for a moment, tears streaming down her cheeks
as she leaves him to cry himself to sleep between night feedings.*

*A few weeks later, her pediatrician expresses some concern
about her baby's slowing weight gain, but cheerfully assures her
that she has just become a 'midnight snack' for her little one and
needs to begin cutting out night feeds so her baby can learn to
sleep through the night. Lydia feels sick to her stomach as she
leaves the doctor's office, but is determined to put her feelings
aside and be a good mother.*

*Lydia experiences some engorgement issues for the first few
nights, but the discomfort is nothing compared with her
heartbreak at listening to her baby cry. Over the next few weeks,
she notices a perceptible decrease in the volume of her breasts,
and her let-down reflex feels weak. Her fears are confirmed
when she takes her baby back to the pediatrician who is alarmed
to find that Lydia's baby has actually lost weight. Lydia leaves
the pediatrician's office with a diagnosis of failure-to-thrive for
her precious baby, low milk supply for her, and a feeling of utter
failure.*

*At home, Lydia searches for the chic little diaperbag with the
formula samples the hospital provided for her when she brought
her new baby home. She mixes up a bottle, tears falling as she
becomes just another statistic.*

This story about Lydia is being replayed by new mothers across all racial, ethnic, and economic divides. Feeling forced to ignore their natural mothering instincts because of prevailing mainstream parenting practices, these new mothers' levels of anxiety steadily increases in their babies' first weeks, negatively affecting their milk supply. Added to that, nursing on a schedule prevents the mothers from receiving the stimulation of milk production inherent in the frequent suckling of a baby allowed to nurse on demand. Then, the breastfeeding coffin is sealed when night nursing is ended and with it the loss of hours and hours of milk stimulation. The result is seen in the modern epidemic--low milk supply.

The tragedy is not just mothers unable to continue breastfeeding when they deeply desire to, as heartbreaking as that is, but also the loss of health benefits that come with breastfeeding for both infants and breastfeeding mothers. A reduction in the risk of SIDS, asthma, childhood leukemia, diabetes, gastroenteritis, otitis media (ear infections), LRTIs (pneumonia, bronchitis, etc), necrotizing enterocolitis, and obesity are just some of the protective benefits for babies.[5] For mothers, breastfeeding has been correlated with a significant decrease in the risk of diseases such as breast cancer, ovarian cancer, diabetes, and heart disease to name just a few[5].

Additionally, the *Journal of the American Academy of Pediatrics* released a study in April of 2010 that concluded, "The United States incurs $13 billion in excess costs annually and suffers 911 preventable deaths per year because our breastfeeding rates fall far below medical recommendations.[5]" And those numbers are only based on breastfeeding benefits for the first six months of life. The World Health Organization, American Academy of Pediatrics, Centers for Disease Control, and others recommend breastfeeding for the first *two years* of a child's life. Imagine the tally if the researchers had looked at the lives lost and billions of dollars spent unnecessarily in a two year breastfeeding scenario instead of a six month scenario!

The bottom line is this, if you want to breastfeed, get support. Call your local La Leche League. Go online and look for support communities like Best for Babes and KellyMom.com. Don't wait until you're in a desperate situation. Get that support system in place *before* you need it. You'll be amazed at how much easier it will be if you encounter a problem and you've got like-minded mamas offering advice, encouragement, and experience to help you through!

Chapter 5

Babywearing
a.k.a. Making Your Life Easier

Wearing your baby against your heart is one of the most beautiful and bonding experiences you can have with your little one after giving birth. Studies have even shown that mamas and babies can synchronize their heartbeats with a simple smile! Clearly, wearing your baby within kissing distance, where the slightest tilt of the head brings your smile into focus for your precious new little one, is a wonderful gift of connection that has benefits far, far beyond our understanding!

I have six children, so I can testify to the extreme value of babywearing for being able to continue with a busy life after giving birth to a tiny new person. From attending sports practices to grocery shopping to making dinner to housecleaning, babywearing is a life-saver, not to mention a great source of exercise to get that pre-baby body back!

In addition to the benefits to a busy mama, babywearing can also replace tummy-time[11] for little ones who don't enjoy being stuck on the floor. While being worn, babies' core and neck muscles are being strengthened by the motion of a mother's body while she walks and bends and moves throughout the day.

Also, the incidence of plagiocephaly, or flat-head syndrome, has increased dramatically[6] since the medical community began recommending infants sleep on their backs to reduce the risk of SIDS. While babies should certainly sleep on their backs, they don't need to spend their days in carriers, strollers, bouncers, and swings, or lying flat on their backs on playmats or blankets, which only increase the amount of pressure to a baby's still-flexible skull bones, resulting in a flattened area that may require a helmet to remold it into a normal shape. Babywearing reduces the amount of time infants spend on their backs, thus reducing or even eliminating the risk of plagiocephaly.

Since most babies naturally desire to be close to their source of food and comfort, babies tend to be calmer and more content when being worn than when they are left alone, though there is always that unique baby who likes his or her own space. Babywearing, as with all other options for parenting gently, needs to be adapted to suit a little one's own personality and needs. Some high-needs babies may do better taking naps during the day while being worn, giving mama a hands-free break while still meeting her baby's needs. Other babies do well being worn after nursing to aid in digestion, reducing gassiness and the incidence of reflux.

Babywearing also aids in hip health when using a properly designed carrier. *The International Hip Dysplasia Institute* has warned against excessive amounts of time in car seats, walkers, swings, and other devices that keep babies' legs extended and pushed together. Their recommendation is for a baby's legs to be in the 'frog' position, with their thighs supported and their knees bent.[7] This is the positioning you should look for when shopping for a carrier for your little one.

The options for carriers are truly impressive, but can be a bit overwhelming. If you find yourself lost in a maze of Mei Tais, Ergos, Moby Wraps, and Bobas, check out the links to product reviews and recommendations at littleheartsbooks.com or look for a local baby carrier club or rental service that offers various styles of carriers to try out for yourself. A good choice of carrier will go a long way toward a happy, healthy start in life for your little one and a happier, less stressed mommy, too!

~ Toddler Time ~

Chapter 6

To a Toddler Sharing is a Four Letter Word: MINE

Almost from the moment babies are born, parents teach them not to share. "No, no, sweetie. That's mommy's" and "That's daddy's, not yours" accompanied by the removal of whatever the forbidden item is are daily realities for little ones. This is unavoidable, of course, since bacteria-ridden keys don't belong in little mouths and iPhones don't work well when soaked in drool.

But the challenge comes when our little 'reflectors' are then expected to share their toys with anyone and everyone who takes a liking to them. Keep in mind that 'their toys' as defined by a toddler are anything they own, are playing with, want to play with, don't want to play with but want to remain available, etc. Parents invite other little ones with the same undeveloped sharing abilities over for playdates and then are shocked and embarrassed when the toddler version of wrestle-mania goes down in the playroom.

It's fully acceptable for us adults to not share our 'toys' with others, though. Think about it. How often do we invite friends over and hand them the keys to our car? And yet we get to choose our own friends, do the inviting, and we have adult reasoning skills and judgment in place...things small children don't have control over or access to.

The primary learning mode for little ones is imitation, but still we expect them to somehow have the cognitive maturity to learn to share despite their parents not sharing their 'toys' with them and despite seeing their parents not sharing their 'toys' with their own friends.

On top of that, we're expecting them to grasp some pretty intricate and tricky relational nuances. *What does 'being a good friend' entail? Why is someone taking something I want an acceptable part of friendship? If they can take what I want, why can't I take what they want?*

To round off the difficulty, ownership is an advanced, abstract concept, and sharing is even more so. The difference between sharing and giving away forever or between someone borrowing your things and someone stealing from you is rather nebulous in the mind of a child. Add in a complete inability to grasp time concepts (*They get my toy for a minute? How long is a minute? When mommy tells me 'just a minute' while she's on the phone, it seems like forever before she's done!*). Then add a lack of understanding of other abstract concepts such as permanence, and you can see the murky waters tiny people are expected to navigate when it comes to understanding sharing!

Obviously, little ones need help overcoming all of these obstacles. Punishing them, labeling them as selfish or spoiled brats, forcing them to share, etc. are all counterproductive, not to mention damaging to the very relationship that is pivotal to eventual understanding of the concept of sharing. Going back to that primary learning mode of imitation, the key to teaching a child to share lies in the trust relationship being built by gentle, responsive parenting:

1. When a child is secure in their relationship with their parents, when they know they will be heard, when they trust that their needs will be met quickly and consistently, much of the impetus behind the refusal to share is removed simply because the child isn't living in a constant state of 'fight or flight' response. This is not to say they will share freely, no matter how gentle the parenting. The aforementioned obstacles are still in play, and your little ones are still human. What it does mean is that some

of the impediments to sharing are removed and the stage is set for learning.

2. Within the context of the parent/child relationship, be mindful of how often you say "no" or "mine" and instead try to offer alternatives such as a used gas card in place of a credit card or a play set of keys in place of your car keys in the moment to model sharing.

3. Be aware of the fact that your child isn't choosing their own friends at this point and neither they nor their little playmates are socially skilled yet. Stay nearby and in tune with your little one so you can step in and help them deal with any sharing difficulties such as snatching or tug-o-war with a toy before they escalate.

4. Use clear, kind, concrete words to guide your little one in social situations. For example, try "Use your gentle hands" instead of "Don't snatch/hit/push."

5. Resist the embarrassed-adult-knee-jerk-reaction of scolding your child, snatching toys from them to give to another child, and punishing your child for a normal developmental stage. That kind of reaction not only doesn't model self-control, but it also doesn't model acceptable social behavior, which is exactly what you're upset about your child not displaying!

6. Prepare for playdates by putting away any treasured toys such as special lovies or new toys that you know your little one will have trouble sharing. Honoring their feelings about these few special things will help them to feel more comfortable sharing their other toys because you are showing them in a concrete manner that you will help them to protect and preserve the things that matter to them.

7. Play sharing games with your child daily to practice this advanced skill. When they say "Mine!" respond by smiling, picking up something of yours you don't mind them playing with, and saying, "This is mine. I'll share!" and hand it to them. Often little ones will start running around picking up their toys and bringing them to you to 'share' and wait for it to be

reciprocated, resulting in a back and forth sharing game that taps into another excellent learning mode for children...play!

Above all, keep in mind that sharing is a learned skill and it will take time for your small one to grow into a socially skilled little butterfly. Creating an atmosphere of trust, modeling sharing, and honoring their feelings will surround them with a safe environment in which they can develop the skills needed to become the most treasured of friends.

Chapter 7

Three Simple Steps from Diapers to Potty

I have an adorable little diaper-bottomed twenty-five-month-old who will never be potty-trained. She will, however, in her own time move from diapers to potty as easily as she went from rolling to scooting, from scooting to crawling, from crawling to walking. As a mama of six from twenty-five-years down to twenty-five-months-old, I've supported my little people through the transition to pottying plenty of times, and I've learned to go with the flow.

So, what does 'going with the flow' mean in the diapers-to-potty stage?

- It means no charts, no stickers, no rewards, no punishment, no pressure, no 'training' of any kind.

- It means I don't drive myself nuts looking for signs of 'readiness' or getting frustrated by accidents or worrying about what anyone else thinks.

- It means my children and I are on the same team, period. I don't set my little ones up for a power-struggle, don't shift our relationship from connected to contentious, don't push them to develop according to some arbitrary schedule.

- It means letting my little ones learn about what their bodies can do simply and naturally on their own schedule.

- And it means not ascribing ulterior motives to normal behavior.

Humans have a God-given instinct to seek privacy for the natural process of emptying their bowels, a vital protection against the spread of disease in ancient times. Modern parents, though, often believe a child who seeks a little alone-time to poop is "hiding because they know they're doing something wrong."

That attitude from parents gives children the message that normal bowel functions are somehow shameful and disgusting. That often not only pushes children to seek even more seclusion while pooping, but can also lead to 'holding' behaviors with their resultant medical issues and can actually delay the transition to pottying--the exact opposite effect the parents are trying to achieve.

Also, when asked if they are pooping, small children will frequently deny it and even run away. Parents tend to interpret that as lying and often will punish the child, creating an even more challenging environment for little ones to try to navigate their way from diapers to potty. Again, it is a normal human instinct to regard bowel habits as a private issue, and children are in the unfortunate position of not having the ability to articulate their need for privacy with anything more than a "No!" and a quick getaway.

Parents who recognize that the diapers-to-potty transition is a normal progression of early childhood just like learning to crawl and walk and talk will take the same approach they did with those milestones:

1. Let the child determine the time-table. There is a huge range of 'normal' when it comes to the timing of developmental milestones, including pottying.

2. Encourage, don't push. Just as with rolling, crawling, walking, and other milestones, offering lots of praise and applause without being insistent allows the child to develop at their own pace in a stress-free, supportive environment.

3. Model the desired behavior and offer the opportunity to experiment. Sharing our own experiences with our children is

our most powerful teaching tool, and experimentation is the foundation of true learning.

Remember, the connection we maintain throughout these transitions in our children's lives builds the trust and communication so vital to a healthy parent/child relationship.

Here's what the transition from diapers to potty looks like at our house:

From the time my babies can walk (sometimes even earlier) they regularly join me when I go to the bathroom. They sit on a little potty that's always available or they walk around, familiarizing themselves with this new play-space, and we read books or chat or sing or just hang out.

I occasionally ask if they want to take off their diaper and sit on the little potty, and sometimes they do and sometimes they don't.

Eventually, the day comes that they pee-pee in the potty.

Then, of course, we sing the pee-pee song, "Pee-pee in the po-tay! Pee-pee in the po-tay!" and dance through the house and everybody else joins in and it's a great time.

Sometimes, that one event is kind of an 'ah-ha' moment for my little ones, and the potty games are on! They start asking to go more and more and are usually out of diapers, accident-free, within a couple of weeks. No pressure, no stress, and very little mess.

Sometimes, though, it's a one-off and my little one happily continues in diapers, visiting the bathroom with me off and on, sometimes hanging out on the potty, sometimes not. Then, when they're ready, they let me know and their own potty game is on.

The thing is, barring developmental issues, children *always* eventually make the transition to using the potty and end the diaper-bottomed season of their life. In our home they just do it in their own time. It's as natural and joyous of a developmental milestone as crawling, walking, or talking and, for us, just as celebrated!

Note: There is a rather intense debate in the parenting community over the use and misuse of praising children. While throwing a "Good job" or "Awesome" at a child just to brush them off is, well, a brush off, honestly sharing your excitement and pride in your children is never a bad thing. In our family, we celebrate all 'firsts' with our children, praise their efforts and offer encouragement and help when they're struggling, and admire their accomplishments when they succeed.

Chapter 8

Gentle Weaning

As babies grow from the newborn stage, through infancy, and into the toddler years, there is a natural and healthy progression toward independence that blossoms when a secure trust-foundation is in place. That trust-foundation is forged through the consistent meeting of a baby's needs lovingly, gently, and empathetically by a primary caregiver.

When a baby is breastfed, his mother is naturally close and available and, when parenting by following her maternal instincts, tends to be in tune with her baby in a beautiful symbiosis of unspoken communication. At some point, a baby will begin to 'taste-test' foods, learning through oral exploration about the textures and tastes of foods other than breastmilk. This progresses to a decrease in the need for mommy's milk for nutritional purposes, but is often accompanied by an unexpected and dramatic increase in a little one's demand to nurse which can be quite disconcerting.

Parents have a tendency to assign motives to their children's behavior based on their own childhood experiences and/or their adult perception of the circumstances. In the case of the increased demand for nursing which seems inversely proportional to the need for nursing, the motives parents often assign to their toddlers are that they are "testing" or "pushing their boundaries."

But think of it from the toddler's perspective. They have been gradually moving away from their 'source' of all things, you, and exploring what can be a big, scary world for a little person. No longer are they completely helpless, entirely dependent on another person for everything, but, as their independence has increased, so has their awareness of the world around them and their smallness by comparison. It is at this point that the all-important source of nutrition shifts into a support role, becoming, literally, a touchstone of security. A toddler's increased need to nurse is, in fact, a need for reconnection and reassurance.

Obviously, nursing every five minutes isn't practical and can be downright uncomfortable, especially with the accompanying toddler 'gymnurstics.' This is an excellent time for a parent to learn how to remain in tune with their child as the ages and stages pass with their constantly evolving connection needs. Paying attention to the needs behind the behaviors is an essential element in a healthy parent/child relationship, and, once a little one progresses beyond the basic needs stage, that learning curve can get pretty steep. This is a time when parents can begin experimenting with new ways to engage with their children to meet those reconnection needs in age-appropriate and relationship-building ways, an important skill that will serve parents well in the coming years.

Here are some things to try when faced with a toddler insisting on nursing every few minutes:

- Babywearing is one of my best tools, and I have a sling nearby for any time my toddler seems to need some closeness.

- Reading picture books is also a daily (actually, multiple times a day!) standard at our house, and when my little one toddles up to me, book in hand, I'll plop down on the floor in whatever room I'm in and take a few minutes to read a book and talk about the pretty pictures.

- Cuddling together in the same chair where we typically nurse and instead reading, playing pat-a-cake, watching a movie together, or even offering food or snacks to share, gives them a sense of sameness that is very reassuring.

- Playing games, making silly faces in the mirror, playing dress up together, taking walks, going to the park, anything that assures my toddler that I'm still available to her and enjoy being with her helps to meet the underlying need driving the nursing demands.

- Oddly enough, offering to nurse my toddler several times a day is very reassuring and actually decreases the frequency of the demands!

The main message here is to try different things until you find what works for you and your child, always focusing on staying connected and responsive to your little one's needs. Change can be difficult for both parents and children, but it can be an exciting time, too, as you get to grow with your child into the next stage of life.

Chapter 9

Picky Eater? Here's Help!

I was one of those children who was incredibly picky when it came to food and, despite my mom's gently enforced 'one bite rule,' I went on to become an incredibly picky eater as an adult, as well. I vividly remember as a young child gagging as I tried to force down a bite, my throat feeling like it was closing up, and like there was no way food was going to fit through. As a very compliant child, disappointing my mother bothered me immensely. Being the logical person that I was even at that young age, I remember feeling that her expectations were reasonable and being frustrated at my own inability to comply.

Fast forward a few years to when I began having children of my own and needed to make parenting decisions about everything from breastfeeding to co-sleeping to discipline. On my journey to gentle parenting, I revisited my childhood memories often, finding myself appreciating my mom's gentleness and her way of using silliness to help me see the 'silver lining' in life when things were hard. In some things, I chose to follow the parenting path my mom took, and in others I took a different course and blazed my own trail.

When I was at university, I worked as a certified nutrition consultant with a focus on natural approaches to nutrition, health, and fitness. I took that knowledge, along with my studies in developmental psychology, human behavior, and communication, and incorporated all of it into my parenting decisions.

As I muddled through the toddler years with my firstborn, I decided to take an approach to nutrition that was unheard of, as far as I knew. I would offer to nurse, offer the food on my plate, and offer food I'd made specifically for him, and then let my little man decide. That was the beginning of our baby-led weaning, though I didn't know that term at the time.

What I discovered then and have seen proven time and again through the years with my own six very different children as well as with the families I've worked with, is that, given the freedom to choose, children will generally experiment with more textures and tastes than if they are forced to eat their parents' choice of food for them. It's simply human nature that, if a child (or an adult, for that matter!) knows that they don't *have* to try a new food and that they can run to the trashbin and spit it out if they do try it and don't like it, then they are far, far more likely to give it a chance. And if they don't try it the first time it's offered, or if they do try it and don't like it, making it available again off and on in the future will give them more opportunities to try the food and perhaps end up liking it when their tastes mature a bit more.

In our home, my children know that if they don't like what's being served for a meal there is always an alternative in the form of a PB&J or a reheat later if they just aren't hungry at mealtime. Even if they like the food being served, they may not feel hungry for a heavy meal just then or perhaps the last time they ate that meal their tummy got upset or maybe there are other reasons they don't want the meal that they simply can't articulate. As the adult, I can choose to make an issue out of it and end up in an unnecessary power struggle, or I can choose to offer my children the same respect I offer myself, because you can bet your bottom dollar that if I don't want to eat something, I'm not eating it!

Among the many benefits of this approach, beyond the greater propensity for a child to experiment with tastes and textures and beyond the elimination of mealtime battles, I also saved myself a ton of mommy guilt through the years. I had no way of knowing early on that one of my little ones had Sensory Processing Disorder which was strongly affecting her ability to eat or that another one of my little people was missing an enzyme and couldn't eat meat. Had I spent their toddler years forcing foods on them and engaging in coercive or punitive mealtime parenting, the damage to our relationship, not to mention their health, could have been disastrous. Additionally, children who feel powerless over their lives can begin trying to recapture a sense of power by exercising excessive control over their eating with the danger of a resulting eating disorder when they get into their teen years.

So, on a practical level how do you get a toddler or preschooler to eat? Well, first and foremost, rigidly scheduling mealtimes creates a battleground in and of itself. Toddlers' and preschoolers' ever-shifting growth patterns cause them to go through slow-growth periods where they simply aren't hungry and other periods where they're hungry 24/7. Grazing, or eating multiple small meals and snacks throughout the day, not only fits these growth patterns better, but is actually a much healthier way for all of us to eat. Grazing stabilizes blood sugar which, when low, often leads to overeating; it tends to keep portion sizes smaller; and it increases our awareness of our body's hunger cues. Teaching our little ones to listen to their body's hunger cues is a hugely positive step toward avoiding obesity later in life, as well!

Secondly, a combination of keeping little ones active so they work up a good appetite (which also sets them on the path toward an active physical lifestyle) and offering a variety of healthy foods throughout the day is typically all it takes to meet their nutritional requirements.

As a general guideline, toddlers and preschoolers need:

- Two to three servings of dairy (i.e. 1 oz. cheese, ½ cup milk, ½ cup yogurt);

- Four to six servings of grains (i.e. ½ slice bread, ½ cup non-sugared cereal, ¼ cup pasta, 2 crackers);

- Two servings of protein (i.e. two 1" squares of chicken, fish, or beef);

- Two to three servings of fruit (i.e. ½ banana, apple, orange, etc., ¼ cup raisins, blueberries, raspberries, 3-4 strawberries or grapes);

- Two to three servings of veggies (i.e. 2 tbsp. peas, corn, cauliflower)

  Here are some fun ways to invite your little ones to make healthy eating choices: (*Note: Never feed nuts or honey to a baby under a year old.)

~*Breakfast ideas*~

- Need an easy and healthy breakfast for little ones? Try an ice cream cone filled with almonds & bite sized chunks of fruit and cheese.

- Start a little person's day healthy and happy. Make a smiley face clock on their plate with almonds, cheese, and fruit with yogurt to dip them in.

- Cookies for breakfast! Make 'apple cookies' (apples sliced into round discs) into faces with almonds, raisins, and cheese.

- How about a sundae breakfast? Yogurt sprinkled with granola, raisins, and nuts and drizzled with local honey (helps control seasonal allergies, too). Yummy!

- Here comes the sun! Make frozen pancakes healthier by surrounding them with fruit and topping with berries and almonds and drizzling with local honey!

~*Lunch ideas*~

- Banana Boats ~ Slice of whole wheat bread spread with peanut butter and local honey, wrapped around a banana. Top with just a sprinkle of brown sugar for a treat!

- Double Trouble ~ Celery, carrot and pretzel sticks with a scoop of cottage cheese and a scoop of peanut butter for double dipping!

- Picasso PB&J's ~ Round whole wheat flat bread with small dollops of peanut butter, fruit preserves and yogurt around the edge in a colorful palate with pretzel sticks for paint brushes!

~Dinner ideas~

- Boil some cauliflower, carrots, zucchini, and yellow squash until a bit mushy, then puree.

  1. Mix with your favorite meatloaf recipe for a hidden veggie serving
  2. Mix with spaghetti sauce and freeze in single serving containers.

- Spaghetti Twisters ~ Make rotini noodles instead of spaghetti noodles for a cute 'twist' and add your special spaghetti sauce for a tornado of veggie goodness!

- Pizza Racers ~ Use rectangular flatbread & lightly coat with olive oil and broil for a couple of minutes to crisp it up, then add your souped-up spaghetti sauce & let your little ones top with mozzarella 'racing stripes' & pepperoni 'racing tires' for a super-charged dinner!

- Pureed cauliflower also works great mixed with mac & cheese, stuffing, and mashed potatoes for a hidden veggie to round out any meal!

Chapter 10

Are You a Parent Reject?

Capri points at the front door every morning and says, "Daddy, go!" Her daddy feels a bit rejected, especially on the weekends when he doesn't have to go to work and his little girl cries because he won't leave!

When Daddy and Luca play tickle monsters after bath time, Mommy tries to join in, but Luca grabs Mommy's hand and drags her back to her computer chair. Her mommy feels like she's just the parent workhorse while Daddy gets to be the playmate.

Micah cries and yells, "No-no, Daddy!" when Daddy tries to help with bedtime. Daddy feels like he's missing out on some of the most important memory-making parts of his little guy's childhood.

While these parents' feelings are, of course, valid, the rejection they are feeling is actually a misinterpretation of their children's actions. Small children are creatures of habit. They've only recently arrived in this world and everything is strange and new and big and loud and confusing, so it makes sense that they find comfort and security in repetition and routine. That's the reason they ask us to read the same book to them over and over and over and...well, you get the idea.

As little ones begin to learn and grow, they categorize things in order to understand them. That's why right at first every animal is a 'kitty' and every drink is 'juice.' This same process of learning through categorization applies to relationships, as well. Children are constantly observing and studying their parents and the roles each of them play, and then using that information to construct a mental 'schematic' of their world.

If a child is accustomed to one parent doing the bedtime routine while the other is busy cleaning up after dinner, a sudden change in that routine may disrupt the little one's schematic, and they will often resist or have a meltdown.

Understanding that it is the break in routine, the unexpected happening when a small child has settled in their mind what the 'expected' is, that is at the root of the issue can help a parent to overcome their feelings of rejection and focus on working toward a solution in a way that meets their child's security needs.

Here are five ideas to try if you or your partner are a parent 'reject':

1. When you know a routine is going to change, talk about it with your child ahead of time to prepare them. For instance, if your little one is used to daddy going to work and you have a day off coming up, you can say, "Daddy gets to stay home and play tomorrow!" the evening before and then in the morning, "This is the day I get to stay home and play! What should we do first?"

2. If you'd like to share the diapering duties, but your little one is used to just one parent doing the changes, start by having the non-diapering parent assist for a few changes, then switch roles, but continue to do it together until your baby is comfortable with the new routine.

3. The same ideas apply to bedtime or bath time routines, dropping off or picking up your little one from preschool, or any other routine your child is used to. If you need to change the routine, talk about it ahead of time to prepare them and then try to walk through the routine a few times together before switching roles or sharing the routine.

4. If one parent has a special play time with your little one, instead of trying to join in, why not choose a separate time for the three of you to play together? That will allow them to have a special bonding time for just the two of them while providing an opportunity at another time for you all to bond as a family.

5. Keep in mind that, for very young babies, their survival instinct may make them quite partial to their mommy for the first few months to a year old or even beyond into the toddler years, depending on their personality. That is a natural, normal, and healthy design inbuilt to ensure that they stay attached to their source of food and comfort. If a securely attached baby is having trouble bonding with anyone other than mommy, instead of trying to detach baby, try building your bond while baby is happy and content in mommy's arms. Play peek-a-boo, make fishy-faces, read picture books, and just chat with baby. That will help your little one to begin to associate you with the same safety and comfort they feel in mommy's embrace while building your own secure bond with them.

Chapter 11

Gently Setting Limits

Parenting is soooo tiring and frustrating at times. Sometimes you just want to sit a small child down and say, "Do you know how much easier your life (and mine!) would be if you'd just be REASONABLE?!?" But we know that wouldn't do any good because the words 'reasonable' and 'toddler' or 'preschooler' just don't play well together. The thing to remember is that gentle parenting doesn't mean parenting without boundaries.

Believe it or not, the foundation for discipline (i.e. guiding, leading, teaching…*not* punishment) begins in the newborn and infancy stages. When parents respond quickly, consistently, and gently to their baby's cries, the trust relationship that the parent is establishing becomes the cornerstone for later discipline. Boundaries need to be established for a child's safety and growth into a successful citizen of our world. A child who is secure in the knowledge that he doesn't have to fight to be heard or to have his needs met tends to be more open to and cooperative with limits. And, when the limit-setter is a person the child trusts, the enforcement of those boundaries becomes a matter of connection and communication instead of conflict and struggle.

So, what might setting and enforcing boundaries using gentle parenting look like in real life? Here are a few examples:

- Your eighteen-month-old has begun hitting you whenever you try the 'remove and distract' method of keeping her from sticking things into power outlets. In addition to covering the outlets with safety covers, a gentle parenting approach to hitting at this age would be to gently hold your child's hand when she tries to hit, look her in the eye, and say quietly and firmly, "Gentle," or "Gentle hands," while stroking your cheek with her hand. This sets a boundary that hitting is not okay while demonstrating what behavior is acceptable. Don't expect this to be a one-time deal, though. Little ones learn through consistent and patient repetition.

- Your two-year-old drops to the ground in limp protest every time you try to leave *anywhere*! First, giving a toddler some warning that a change is about to occur respects their often intense interest in and focus on their own activities. A gentle parenting approach might be to utilize the 'countdown to leaving' method to give them a time context (i.e. "Five more minutes! That means you have enough time for five more horsey rides on grandpa's back!"... "Four more minutes! That means you can have four more jumps into the ballpit!"... "Three more minutes! That means you have enough time to build three more towers and knock them down!"... "Two minutes left! That means you have enough time to go down the slide two more times!"... "One more minute! That means you can look at one more book!"). Remember, children aren't little robots we can just upload the right program into and expect it to work perfectly every time, so when your little human still impersonates a limp noodle despite your best efforts, quietly acknowledge his distress, "It's hard to leave when you're having fun, isn't it?" and then gently pick him up go.

- Your three-year-old flat out refuses to wear shoes, period. In addition to giving choices, "Do you want to wear the red boots or the blue sneakers today?" and offering her the opportunity to assert her independence, "Would you like to put your shoes on yourself or do you want mommy to help?" sometimes all that is needed is a simple question, "Why don't you want to wear shoes?" Three-year-olds are typically becoming articulate enough that, if they aren't already stressed, they can do a pretty good job of explaining themselves. You might be surprised to hear something like, "Tomowow my boos hut my toes," which when translated means, "The last time I wore my boots they

hurt my feet, and now I think all shoes will hurt me."
Moving on to a more verbal communication stage of
your relationship with your child when they're ready
might seem a no-brainer, but parents often get caught
up in patterns of parenting from previous stages and it
just doesn't occur to them to simply ask their child
what's wrong. Again, this won't always work, so when
your little bohemian still rejects all things soled, calmly
let her know that she will remain in the
stroller/sling/cart and not do any walking until she
decides she's ready to put on her shoes.

One other note about parental boundaries is that it's not just your
children who will challenge them. Everyone and their mother
will take every 'misbehavior' by your child as an opportunity to
give you unsolicited and often unwanted advice. Remember,
when it comes down to it, it's you, the parent, who determines
what limits to set.

In practical application, boundaries do reflect the culture and
environment in which a child lives. In a small, rural community
in Spain, doors may be left open day and night and the neighbors
may all be related. Small children might have the freedom to
wander in and out of houses, play ball in the middle of the road,
and plop down for an afternoon nap on a neighbor's sofa. In a
busy, urban city such as New York, doors may be kept locked,
people may never have even met their neighbors, and letting a
child play in the street might be tantamount to a child
endangerment charge.

The point is that boundaries aren't a one-size-fits-all list that you
can buy from Barnes & Noble, put on the fridge, and slap a
sticker on every time a child complies. Boundaries are personal
limits determined by the parents' values and priorities and
culture as well as reflecting the age and maturity of their child
and the unique attributes of their community.

It may 'take a village' to raise a child, but remember, it's you,
the parent, who's the leader of your tribe!

~ A Preschooler with a Plan ~

Chapter 12

My Little Caboose and the Very Bad, No Good...Month

My adorable little five-year-old has been a royal pain in the caboose for the last few weeks. She has whined, cried, ignored direct requests, climbed on me, hung on me, played with her food, snatched things from the baby, been in my face and space incessantly, and on and on and on. And the more difficult she got, the more I 'powered up' on her. Oh, I didn't yell or punish. No, I pulled out all of my gentle parenting techniques, spoke calmly and respectfully to her, offered diversions and alternatives, read her books and provided lots of reasonable and kind council. She occasionally responded with a half-hearted attempt at cooperation or humorously declined to cooperate, but more often than not just dug in her heels and determinedly upset the normally peaceful and happy timbre of our home.

And then it happened.

A few nights ago, I stood in the shower listening to the goings-on outside the door (A mama's ears are the proverbial 'eyes in the back of her head' you know!), and it hit me. Over and over, I heard my older children tell my little caboose, "No," as she made one unfortunate decision after another. Over and over, I heard her whine and argue and cry. Over and over, I heard the older ones correct her, not hatefully or harshly, but repeatedly, gently, and firmly. And, over and over, I realized I was hearing myself as my older children reflected what they were seeing and hearing from me...repeated, gentle, firm correction...but no listening...none.

And my heart broke.

I realized that I had been parenting from a position of disconnect from my precious little caboose. Between jumping through all the hoops necessary to get a homeschooler into a pre-med university program to working with my publisher on the super slow and cumbersome process of getting my book released, to writing an upcoming children's book series, my busy schedule had overtaken my parenting.

How many times had I told my little caboose, "Just a minute," when she needed me? How often had that 'minute' stretched into an hour? How many times had my eyes strayed back to my computer screen in the middle of one of her stories about how terribly painful the invisible scratch on her pinky toe was or how pretty the light looked as it danced through the dust motes in front of the window? How often had she fallen asleep waiting, waiting, waiting for me to come and read her a bedtime story? (Oh, my mama's heart hurts.)

And so I took my own advice, the advice I've given umpteen times to other mama's who were experiencing a 'parenting disconnect.' I took my disgruntled, whiney, clingy, disruptive child (who I felt like sending to her room just so I could have a break!) and I pulled her closer than close, under my mama's wing. I took her everywhere with me. I let her sleep on a pallet next to my bed. We cooked dinner together and made a museum out of her paintings and folded towels together. And I listened and listened and listened, intentionally and thoughtfully and responsively. And my little caboose and I reconnected. In just a matter of days, life in our household returned to its normal cadence of what we affectionately call 'joyful chaos.'

People see the difference and ask me, "What did you do?" and I simply respond, "I listened."

Here's a little story to illustrate...

The little caboose chugged along day after day, clickety-clack, clickety-clack, happy as could be as she followed her mama engine and brother and sister cars along the tracks. Up and down hills, around curves and through tunnels they went, all strung together with their secure couplings. At the end of each day, they headed back to the station to get all fueled up and rested for the next glorious day.

One day, the little caboose was startled when mama engine took off extra early without checking to make sure all the couplings were tightened. As they chugged forward, the little caboose could feel her coupling slipping a bit, and she "choo-chooed" loudly to get mama engine's attention. But mama engine was too busy to notice and kept picking up speed as they began their journey up and down the hills.

Alarmed, little caboose tried to pull backwards and slow the train down, but mama engine chugged on, "choo-chooing" encouragingly. Little caboose felt her coupling getting looser and looser as mama engine sped toward the dangerous curves and tunnels ahead. In a panic, little caboose screeched "choo-choo" over and over and tugged and pulled backward frantically. Mama engine just chugged on, this time "choo-chooing" firmly and giving a gentle extra tug forward.

Little caboose spent the rest of the day screeching "choo-choo" and pulling and tugging backward until they finally arrived back at the station, everyone exhausted and cranky from the difficult day. Little caboose was so overwrought from the fear of being disconnected all day that she continued to screech "choo-choo" and pull at her coupling even after they were stopped for the night.

Mama engine chugged ominously in her direction, determined to restore order, but suddenly paused, hearing for the first time the fear and exhaustion in her little caboose's "choo-choos." She looked carefully and noticed the loose coupling.

Pulling little caboose closer than close, mama engine tightened the coupling and "choo-chooed" a soft, reassuring lullaby, and little caboose finally stopped her screeching and tugging and relaxed, gratefully snuggling into her mama engine's familiar, safe embrace.

The Challenge

If you have a parenting issue right now, any parenting issue at all for any age child, take a mental snapshot of what a typical day looks like at the moment. Then take one week, just a single week out of your life, and listen to your child.

Listen intentionally. Listen consciously. Create opportunities for your child to talk. Open conversations to get them started, then stop talking and stop planning your response and stop mentally going over your to-do list and just listen.

Take your child with you whenever you can, wherever you're going. Involve them in your day. Invite them into your life.

Enjoy them and get to know them, get to really know the unique and remarkable person they are. They are a precious, priceless gift, and their childhood will be over before you know it.

At the end of the week, take another mental snapshot of what a day with your child looks like. Then you can decide which path to take.

Will you go backward or forward? Is connecting with your child worth your time and effort? What will you choose?

Chapter 13

The Problem with Punishment

Want to know a dirty, little secret about punishment?

It doesn't work.

Punishment may be able to control a child's *behavior* temporarily while they're small or when they are in their parents' presence, but it cannot control the *person*. As with all humans, outward behavior is merely a reflection of our inner selves: our needs, our hurts, our emotional states.

While the temporary 'payoff' of punishment may be compliance, the need behind the behavior is never addressed and those needs merely get driven underground and often emerge later in more potentially damaging behaviors such as lying, sneaking, anger, outright rebellion, depression, aggression, addictions, etc.

In the same way that treating a brain tumor by merely taking a pain reliever doesn't address the underlying issue, masking the symptoms of an underlying need with punishment-induced compliance doesn't solve the problem; it intensifies it.

Want to know another dirty, little secret about punishment?

It requires constant escalation.

In order to maintain the temporary effect of controlling behavior, the punishment, or threats of punishment, must constantly be ramped up. Parents who start out with popping a tiny hand escalate to smacking a chubby little leg, then paddling a small bottom. Over time, as their children's needs which have been driven underground emerge in ever-increasing behavioral issues, parents often find that they are resorting to yelling and threats and physical punishment more and more often.

Even parents who use punishment-based parenting approaches other than physical punishment find that they must escalate and escalate to keep their children under 'control.' Behavior charts, time-outs, grounding, and removing privileges are some examples of non-physical punishment-based parenting. While these behavior modification techniques may be less painful to children physically, they still don't address the underlying needs being communicated by the behavior and often are nearly as destructive to the parent/child relationship.

Using isolation such as time-outs or sending children to their room separates them from their source of guidance and comfort just when they need it the most and not only misses a golden opportunity to help the child learn coping mechanisms for dealing with their emotions, but also fractures the very connection that should provide the safety for expressing those emotions. Using behavior charts, removal of privileges, grounding, etc. separates children from their parents by creating an us-against-them mentality that inevitably leads to conflict instead of creating a teamwork mentality that leads to cooperation.

Here's the thing, effective parenting, and effective *discipline* specifically, don't require punishment. Equating discipline with punishment is an unfortunate, but common misconception. The root word in *discipline* is actually *disciple* which in the verb form means to guide, lead, teach, model, and encourage. In the noun form *disciple* means one who embraces the teaching of, follows the example of, and models their life after.

On the flip side, the root word in *punishment* is the Latin word *punire* which in verb form means to penalize, chastise, castigate, inflict harm, humiliate. There is no noun form of *punire* or its English equivalent, *punishment*.

Many of today's most popular self-proclaimed parenting 'experts' equate physical punishment with discipline and go to great lengths to describe the best methods and tools for hitting children as well as instructing parents to maintain a calm, controlled, and even cheerful demeanor as they 'lovingly' hit their children.

It is interesting to note here that, when it comes to the law, crimes of passion are treated as less heinous than premeditated, planned, and purposefully executed crimes which are termed 'in cold blood.' And yet when physically punishing a child, a crime in many places across the globe, hitting in anger or frustration (i.e. passion) is deemed wrong by proponents of spanking, while hitting children with calm and deliberate intent (i.e. premeditation) is encouraged.

It is also interesting to note that, in the not-too-distant past, husbands hitting their wives was also viewed as not only a societal norm, but also a necessary part of maintaining a harmonious, successful marriage. In fact, a man who epitomizes the words calm and controlled, Sean Connery, shared his thoughts on the 'reasonable smacking' of his wife in a 1987 interview with Barbara Walters in which he explained the necessity of using punitive methods to control women.[8]

The core belief behind 'reasonable smacking' of wives was that there was no other effective way to control them. I agree. If controlling another human being is the goal, then force is necessary. Fear, intimidation, threats, power-plays, physical pain, those are the means of control.

But, if growing healthy humans is the goal, then building trust relationships, encouraging, guiding, leading, teaching, and communicating are the tools for success.

Many parents simply don't know what else to do. They were raised with spanking and other punishment-based parenting methods as a means of control and "turned out okay" so they default to their own parents' choices without researching alternatives to spanking or considering whether "okay" could be improved upon.

Consider this, more than 90% of American parents admit to spanking their children, and yet the common contention is that it's a decline in spanking that is responsible for the purportedly escalating rates of youth violence and crime. Is it really the less than 10% of children who aren't spanked who are responsible for all the problems of our society? Or could it be that the 90%

of children who are subject to violence at home in the form of being slapped, paddled, smacked, yanked, whipped, popped, spanked, etc. are taking those lessons out into the world? Is it just possible that children who are hit learn to hit? That children who are hurt learn to hurt? Perhaps the lesson they are learning is that 'might is right' and violence is the answer to their problems, the outlet for their stress, the route to getting others to do what they want.

People throughout history have complained about 'the trouble with kids today' and they've pinned all the ills of their society on supposedly permissive parenting. They've ranted about out-of-control children, disrespectful youth, entitlement, spoiling, disobedience, violence, self-centeredness, etc:

"The children now love luxury. They have bad manners, contempt for authority, they show disrespect to their elders.... They no longer rise when elders enter the room. They contradict their parents, chatter before company, gobble up dainties at the table, cross their legs, and are tyrants over their teachers."
~Socrates, 5th Century BC

"What is happening to our young people? They disrespect their elders, they disobey their parents. They ignore the law. They riot in the streets inflamed with wild notions. Their morals are decaying. What is to become of them?"
~Plato, 5th Century BC

"I see no hope for the future of our people if they are dependent on frivolous youth of today, for certainly all youth are reckless beyond words... When I was young, we were taught to be discreet and respectful of elders, but the present youth are exceedingly wise [disrespectful] and impatient of restraint"
~Hesiod, 8th Century BC

"The world is passing through troublous times. The young people of today think of nothing but themselves. They have no reverence for parents or old age. They are impatient of all restraint. They talk as if they knew everything, and what passes

for wisdom with us is foolishness with them. As for the girls, they are forward, immodest and unladylike in speech, behavior and dress."
~Peter the Hermit, 13th Century AD

Sounds familiar, doesn't it? Maybe, though, there isn't really any 'trouble with kids today.' Maybe the problem is with parents who repeat the patterns their own parents set or with societies who view normal stages of development as somehow abnormal.

Maybe 'kid's today' are just kids like they have been through the ages, full of exuberance and curiosity and learning their way in a great big world, and a listening ear, gentle guidance, and trusted arms to turn to when inevitable mistakes are made are really all children need to grow up into kind, helpful, responsible, productive members of our society.

The bottom line is that addressing our children's underlying needs, the actual causes of their behavior instead of just the behavior itself, is a far more effective parental approach as well as being significantly better for a healthy, mutually respectful parent/child relationship. Sending our children out into the world as adults with their needs met, with coping mechanisms in place for those times when the stresses overwhelm them, and with the knowledge of a safe haven where comfort is always available when the world hurts them is a powerful way to change the world for the better.

Maybe, just maybe, sowing peace in our homes is the answer for our children, our families, and our world, after all.

Chapter 14

Age of Fear:
Helping Children Cope with Anxiety

Your once fearless five-year-old suddenly refuses to leave your
side at the park saying, "I'm afraid the birds will eat me," while
eyeing the tiny swallows hopping on the ground as if they're evil
geniuses plotting his demise.

Your three-year-old, whom you once found proudly grinning
while sitting atop the refrigerator, has abruptly decided the
swings are objects of abject terror that will, "Fly me to the
ground." (Translation: I'll fall off!)

Your six-year-old who has slept like a log in his own bed for
years is suddenly resisting bedtime and climbing into your bed
with you at 3 a.m. every. single. night.

Your happy little four-year-old suddenly becomes withdrawn
and clingy, refusing to play with her playdate friends and
wanting to sit in your lap. And, even worse, she's started sucking
her thumb again!

The preschool and early elementary school years are sometimes
marred with exaggerated fears, odd anxieties, nightmares, night
terrors, and other evidences of insecurity that can make the most
confident of parents feel a combination of dismay, frustration,
worry, and failure. Regression is a common accompaniment,
from pottying accidents to night-waking to thumb-sucking.
Often, acting-out behaviors also increase in this time period.

So, what in the world is going on?

No, it's not an environmental-toxin-induced, super-early-onset
of adolescent-hormone-overload. And, normally, it's not a
trauma-reaction to life changes such as moving or starting
preschool or school, though those events can exacerbate the

issue. (Be aware that these behaviors can, rarely, indicate an anxiety disorder, stress-overload, or abuse. If you suspect any of these things may be causing your child's behavior, seek a professional evaluation.)

Typically, though, sudden anxiety behaviors in preschool/early elementary aged children are simply another normal stage of development, an indication of cognitive growth. In other words, as odd as it sounds, fear can be a sign of maturity!

Children in the three- to six-year-old age range (Keep in mind that this is a rough age estimate. Children are individuals, not pre-programmed robots!) are beginning to realize that their parents aren't the all-powerful beings that they once believed them to be. This realization can be very uncomfortable for them, causing them a great deal of unease as they are concurrently beginning to realize that there is a whole, big, wide world beyond their safe, little home, and that that world is full of potential dangers, hazards unknown, and just a lot of really big, scary things.

So what is a parent to do with their newly timid little house-mouse?

First, be aware that there is no one-size-fits-all miracle 'cure.' You know your child better than anyone else, and being responsive to her unique needs means taking your cues from her as to what may help or hinder her journey through this uncomfortable stage.

That said, here are some ideas that may help:

- Before forcing your child to 'face his fears,' consider whether someone throwing a spider on you if you are deathly afraid of spiders or locking you in a closet if you're claustrophobic would be helpful to you in overcoming your fears. If the answer is "NO!" then honor your child's feelings and move on to another solution.

- When your child voices her concerns, resist the urge to minimize them. If she says, "I'm afraid of monsters coming in my window," try not to say, "There's no such thing as monsters." Remember, she's realizing you aren't all-powerful, and that means you aren't all-knowing, either! Rather than be reassured by your words, she'll simply think you don't know about the monsters and can't help her and keep her safe. Instead, you can brainstorm ideas together to keep the monsters at bay. While you don't want to say that monsters actually do exist, you can say something like, "Let's think of ways to keep you safe. What if daddy throws the monsters away in the trashcans outside and the garbage truck takes them away?" Don't be afraid to be seriously silly. In other words, take her fears seriously, but offer silly solutions that offer visuals of the monsters (or whatever the fear is) going away forever.

- Help your child to make a 'nightmare safe' out of a shoe box. At night before he goes to bed, sit with him and encourage him to put all his scary thoughts in the box for you to take and keep safely away from him while he sleeps. Let him know that if he does have a bad dream, he can come to you even if it's the middle of the night, and you'll help him to put the scary dream in the box so he'll be able to go back to sleep.

- Avoid phrases such as "You're a big boy now" and "Only babies do that." Focus instead on encouraging your child to do the things you know he can do. For instance, if he's usually able to climb the ladder on the slide but gets 'stuck' halfway up and asks for help, start by moving near so he knows you are close and willing to help him if needed. Then verbally encourage him, "I know you can do it. I'm here if you need me." But don't pressure him. If he gets upset or insists he can't do it, help him down. Remember, it isn't really about the slide at all. It's about seeking reassurance that you can still be trusted to take care of him, that he's still safe with you.

- If the occasional monster in the closet or under the bed needs to be evicted, try reading a book like *Go Away, Big Green Monster!* and make your own 'Monster-Away Spray,' to send all the scary monsters packing. Role-playing with children (and just playing with them, period) is a powerful tool in helping them learn coping skills, so try pretending to be a monster and let your little one spritz you while you run away squealing, then spray a bit under the bed and in the closet before bedtime to roust the beasties so your little one can sleep in peace.

- If regression is an issue, keep in mind that your child is self-comforting by returning to a time she felt safe. Rather than punishing, ridiculing, bribing, or in other ways trying to 'control' the behavior, offer comfort in appropriate ways to demonstrate that she can trust you to meet her comfort/safety needs. This applies to acting-out behaviors, as well. Set boundaries, certainly, and provide plenty of guidance, but remember that punishment pushes children farther away rather than connecting with them. Since your child is reacting to a feeling of disconnection from you in her new understanding of your non-superhero status, pushing her further away will merely exacerbate the issue, not solve it.

- Just listen. This is the simplest solution to a rather complex problem. Slow down and make time to just take a walk with your child. Sit with him in the evening and watch him color or play a quiet board game with him. Lay with him in his bed for a few minutes before he sleeps and chat about the day. Just taking the time to focus on him, to be quiet with him, to enjoy his company, and to reconnect with him will go a long way towards soothing his fears.

Chapter 15

Bucket List for a Happy Childhood

Let's pack happiness into our children so the baggage they take into adulthood is goodness, confidence, and kindness instead of packing bags of hurt, struggle, and loneliness that will weigh them down for life. The late Barbara Johnson, author of numerous books including *Stick a Geranium in Your Hat and Be Happy*, once wrote, "To be in your children's memories tomorrow, you have to be in their lives today." In our busy, modern lifestyles, it's important to not only be in our children's lives, but also to be intentional about making our time together count in the small ways that really matter to children.

Here are two hundred ways to pack our children's precious and all-too-brief moments of childhood with happiness:

1. Float boats in puddles
2. Ride bikes
3. Play hopscotch
4. Blow dandelions
5. Jump in a bounce house
6. Take them to a museum
7. Play hot-potato with water balloons
8. Make a volcano
9. Buy them a goldfish
10. Have funoodle sword fights
11. Take silly pictures with them in a photo booth
12. Fix pancakes for dinner
13. Let them climb trees
14. Watch your language
15. Make daisy chains
16. Play board games and let them win so they'll feel smart
17. Teach them manners by being polite to them
18. Teach them respect by showing them respect
19. Look at them when they're talking
20. Build block towers and knock them down together

21. Read to them
22. Laugh at their jokes
23. When they're upset say, "I'm here. I'm listening," and then just be there
24. Go barefoot in the grass
25. Thank them sincerely for muddy bouquets of weeds
26. Pray for them
27. Pray with them
28. Tell them the truth
29. Have wrestling matches and let them win so they'll feel strong
30. Let them believe in miracles
31. Let them see you stand up for what you believe in
32. Tickle them and stop when they tell you to so they'll know how to tell someone "No!" when they don't want to be touched
33. Turn off the television
34. Have a picnic on the living room floor
35. Make shadow puppets
36. Let them become best friends with their grandparents (or adopt a grandparent!)
37. Build forts
38. Let them help you fix the toilet
39. Let them jump in piles of clean laundry
40. Take them with you when you vote
41. Have staring contests
42. Make playing-card buildings
43. Make a refrigerator box rocket and fly to Mars for dinner with them
44. Fingerpaint with them
45. Fingerpaint on them
46. Let them fingerpaint on you
47. Tell them corny jokes
48. Blow bubbles
49. Jump in puddles
50. Play football in the mud
51. Play basketball in the driveway at midnight
52. Play baseball at the park
53. Go to their teddy bear tea parties
54. Play with slinkies on the stairs
55. Let them teach you something

56. Put band aids on invisible boo-boos
57. Scare away the monsters
58. Sing in the car
59. Make silly faces in the mirror
60. Roll in piles of leaves
61. Turn off the computer
62. Dance in the rain
63. Make snow angels (or sand angels!)
64. Let them help you help someone in need so they'll learn to serve
65. Make mudpies
66. Cook dinner together
67. Go stargazing
68. Lay in the grass
69. Go fishing with real worms
70. Look for four-leaf clovers
71. Walk in the woods
72. Spot shapes in the clouds
73. Dress up and take them on a date to the symphony
74. Visit a planetarium
75. Give them bear hugs
76. Give them grace
77. Share a secret
78. Tell them about God
79. Tell them stories about your childhood
80. Get them a kitten
81. Visit an aquarium
82. Take them to the zoo
83. Take them to the library
84. Let them meet an author or a painter or an astronaut
85. Let them dream big dreams
86. Admire their artwork
87. Make macaroni art together
88. Go to a sunrise service on Easter
89. Plant something together and watch it grow
90. Go to a Passion play
91. Go to a parade
92. Play dress up
93. Go to the beach
94. Hike up a mountain trail

95. Ride a bicycle-built-for-two (or three!)
96. Hold them when they cry
97. Forgive them when they mess up
98. Help them when they struggle
99. Encourage them to try again when they fail
100. Let them choose the movie
101. Listen to their endless stories
102. Clap when they sing you a song
103. Share a giant bucket of popcorn at the movies
104. Rent a projector and hang up a sheet outside to make your own drive-in theater
105. Take them to an airshow
106. Take them to a Veteran's Day parade and let them shake hands with a hero
107. Tie a towel into a cape and play superheroes
108. Make Christmas cards for nursing home residents and deliver them together
109. Throw a surprise half-birthday party
110. Climb on the furniture and jump over the lava
111. Make a paper mâché globe
112. Make paper airplanes and have a fly-off
113. Fly kites
114. Make sandcastles (or snowmen!)
115. Give butterfly kisses
116. Give Eskimo kisses
117. Go to a petting zoo and let them pet a goat
118. Play jump rope
119. Go to their plays
120. Go to their games
121. Teach them chess
122. Play twister
123. Let them see you reading
124. Go to storytimes at bookstores
125. Go to a farmer's market
126. Make s'mores
127. Camp in the backyard
128. Cook over a campfire
129. Build a model airplane
130. Make up a secret handshake
131. Wear the macaroni necklaces they make you

132. Smile when they walk in the room
133. Kiss them goodbye whenever you leave
134. Dress up for their tea parties
135. Play rock-paper-scissors
136. Say please
137. Say thank you
138. Say you're welcome
139. Tell them you trust them
140. Tell them they are good
141. Tell them you love them every day
142. Say, "I like you"
143. Say, "You're fun to be with"
144. Tell them you miss them when you're away from them
145. Tell them they can always count on you and then be there when they need you
146. Tell them about times you've failed so they know they don't have to be perfect
147. Catch fireflies in jars and then let them go
148. Forgive them so they'll learn to forgive
149. Give second chances, third chances, fourth chances…
150. Race them to the car and let them win so they'll feel success
151. Teach them how to skip rocks
152. Use your gentle hands
153. Stand up to bullies for them
154. Tell them what you believe in
155. Tell them you believe in them
156. Treat them like they're priceless so they'll never doubt their value
157. Let them hear you whistle while you work so they'll know joy can be found in everything
158. Grab a stick for a sword and slay dragons with them
159. Catch ladybugs on your fingers and examine their spots
160. Share a milkshake
161. Have a sleepover in their room
162. Go on a scavenger hunt
163. Give them a hammer, nails, and scrap wood and watch the magic
164. Work puzzles together that take weeks to finish
165. Make grape popsicles and eat them together in the sunshine

166. Be kind to them so they'll learn to be kind

167. Admit it when you're wrong so they'll learn to take responsibility for their actions

168. Say you're sorry when you mess up so they'll learn it's okay to make mistakes

169. Let them see you cry so they'll know it's okay to be human

170. Tell them you're on their side

171. Turn off your cell phone

172. Build a birdhouse together and let them paint it all the colors of the rainbow

173. Help them with their homework so they can play outdoors

174. Play with them

175. Sprinkle fairy dust on their bed to help them sleep

176. Let them see you rescue a butterfly caught in a spider's web so they'll think you're a hero

177. Tell them about the pot of gold at the end of the rainbow and help them search for it

178. Sit on the porch and wave at the passing cars with them

179. Take a ride on a train

180. Take them to see an alligator

181. Read the funny paper in the newspaper to them

182. Let them take care of you when you're sick

183. Listen so they'll learn to listen

184. Care about what they care about so they'll feel understood

185. Put others first so they learn sacrifice

186. Help a neighbor so they'll understand community

187. Let them climb into bed with you when they have a bad dream

188. Make them a cozy reading nook

189. Squeeze yourself into their reading nook and cuddle up for storytime

190. Read them fairy tales

191. Buy them comic books

192. Make paper-chains for the Christmas tree

193. Have a birthday party for Jesus before opening presents on Christmas morning

194. Make blessing bags and mail them to our troops

195. Build bookshelves and start a home library for them

196. Treat them with compassion so they'll learn to care

197. Give them piggyback rides to bed

198. Read them bedtime stories (and let them choose the book even if it's the same one every night!)

199. Show them you love them when they deserve it the least

200. Live what you want them to learn

Chapter 16

Mommy Guilt:
The Human Factor

One of the inherent pitfalls in gentle parenting is the tendency to blame our parenting for any behavior issues our children are having. Screaming baby? Mommy isn't feeding or holding baby enough. Tantruming toddler? Daddy isn't paying close enough attention to his little guy's attempts to communicate. Stubborn preschooler? Mommy isn't offering her sweet girl enough choices.

While it is true that our parenting choices have immediate and long-term impacts on our children, it is vital that we remember that our little mini-me's aren't simply mirrors of our parenting. Our children are separate individuals from ourselves, entirely whole people with wants and needs and hopes and fears and interests and emotions all their own, not to mention their own distinct temperaments and personalities. They can be irritable or contrary or temperamental without it having anything to do with us, at all!

Growth, change, learning, etc. can all be uncomfortable experiences at times, and even as adults we don't always react with calm cooperation to being stretched outside of our comfort zone. The very humanness of our human nature dictates that we don't always respond to our world harmoniously, no matter how kind or empathetic the people who populate our world are.

Our children are just as capable of reacting with irritability to a change in the weather or to a growth spurt as they are to a parenting misstep which is perfectly normal as long as those missteps are the exception rather than the rule. And they are just as likely to challenge the laws of nature (like gravity!) as they are to resist parental boundaries. And, actually, resistance to the way things are can be a wonderful thing…invention and innovation are created by people who aren't satisfied with the status quo, after all.

While there is always room for improvement in our parenting (after all, we're human, too) and being open to growth and evolving as parents is important, remaining in-tune with and responsive to our little ones means being aware of their individuality as much as being cognizant of our connectedness.

Feeding, holding, humming, bouncing, walking, and otherwise soothing our babies and meeting their needs is essential to developing a healthy trust relationship, but internalizing a sense of self-blame during those inevitable times when our soothing and meeting needs doesn't result in a calm, happy baby is destructive and can result in hidden resentment toward our little ones.

Likewise, listening to, playing with, and being flexible with our toddlers and preschoolers are all vital to creating a secure foundation from which they can venture forth and explore the world. But when our efforts don't produce an endlessly-happy, always-confident, perfectly-reasonable child, we can make the mistake of feeling like a failure as a parent instead of simply acknowledging that we are the parent of a human being with all of the normal quirks and foibles inherent in human nature.

This self-blame can be damaging in many ways, from causing the aforementioned resentment to inflicting crushing feelings of inadequacy to creating outright depression in a parent. The result can be a strained or adversarial parent/child relationship filled with misunderstandings, conflict, and anger.

We need to always keep in mind that parenting isn't just a matter of applied techniques with predictable responses. In other words, we aren't programming little robots!

Our little humans are always watching, always learning, always imitating us, and they are as unpredictable as falling stars.

If we continually shoulder the responsibility for our children's behavior, we are not only depriving them of the dignity of taking personal responsibility for themselves, but we are also denigrating their capabilities and individuality, in essence telling them that they simply aren't able to make their own decisions, control themselves, or function without assistance.

And, hear me on this, even if we don't verbally express the belief that their behavior is our fault, if we believe that to be true, then we will express that to them in innumerable, subtle ways that they *won't* miss.

Do we really want to turn our little imitators into blame-shifters who never take responsibility for their own actions? Or can we respect them enough to acknowledge that it really isn't *all* about us--our parenting, our successes, our failures--and that maybe, sometimes, our little one is just having a human moment?

When we've done our parental best, tried our hardest, met needs, cuddled, soothed, played, listened, and guided, and our babies still cry or our children still have that meltdown or make an unfortunate choice, let's simply stay close, calmly offering our comforting arms, reassuring presence, and unconditional love, all the while resting in the peaceful assurance that our little humans are just being...human!

Chapter 17

A Place to Rest: Becoming Our Children's Safe Harbor

"We make children work for our love instead of resting in it. We make them work at keeping us close. Well, we might get more compliance but we get a deeply restless child. And we're giving rise to a whole generation of children who are restless to the core. They do not know how to rest." ~ Gordon Neufeld, PhD, *Relationship Matters.* [9]

Giving our children rest means being their safe harbor, their place to retreat when life hurts and the world looms large and people disappoint and mistakes are made. Becoming that safe harbor means being free ~ freely available, freely offered, freely welcoming.

Imagine a ship damaged at sea, broken and sinking fast, heading for the safety and shelter of the harbor only to be stopped at the end of the breakwaters, the line between storm-tossed sea and calm waters, and told to clean up their deck, fix their rudders, and examine their ship logs to see where they went wrong, all while still in danger of sinking in the rough seas.

Now imagine a child, roughed up by his own bad choices or suffering at the hands of her own human weaknesses, hoping to find a safe harbor in a parent's healing embrace, but instead being sent to isolation in a corner or in their room and told to think about what they've done and pull themselves together before being admitted back into the family.

When we send children to their rooms as punishment or to think about what they've done, we are leaving them all alone in a stormy sea of human emotions when what they really need in that moment is to reconnect with us. They need our wisdom and guidance and the reassurance that, no matter what mistakes they make, no matter how badly they fail, no matter how far they fall, we will always, *always* be there to help them and heal them and forgive them and love them. That is the heart of gentle parenting.

Chapter 18

Death of a Butterfly:
Helping Children Cope with Loss

My little mud-magnet accidentally killed a butterfly while trying to catch its buttery-yellow beauty in her small, cupped hands. Her sweet little heart is broken, and we're walking through the stages of mourning together as I use these small (to us adults) losses to equip her with healthy tools for handling the difficult things life will surely bring through the years, as it does to all of us.

Whether it's the death of a butterfly, the loss of a favorite stuffed animal, or another loss that matters to them deeply, guiding children through their uncomfortable and often overwhelming emotions is something parents are often unprepared to handle.

Here are the steps we take together when life gets hard and loss becomes a reality to my children:

1. *Feeling* ~ The first step is simply allowing my children to feel their emotions. If they're crying, I listen to their cues to know when to offer hugs or if they need some time alone or just someone to sit quietly next to them. If they're angry, I watch closely to see if they need some directions for a safe outlet such as punching a pillow or going outside to kick a ball or if they are able to just stomp around and get it out that way. If they are unnaturally quiet, I let them know I'm there if they need me and then I give them some space to sort through their emotions in their own time.

2. *Expressing* ~ The second step is guiding my children to express their feelings in some tangible form. This step begins either when they initiate a conversation about the loss or when I see that their emotions are getting the best of them, indicating that they need some assistance in moving forward. This step

may take the form of simply talking through what they are feeling, but typically it includes drawing a picture, making up a song or writing or dictating a poem for me to write down for them, making a memory box, or some combination of each of them.

3. *Refocusing* ~ The third and last step is giving my children ideas about how to move on. It's often hard for them to figure out how to redirect their thoughts from constantly swirling around their loss. It takes a measure of mental maturity to be able to focus elsewhere when emotions are running high. This is not to say that they should never think about their loss again. I am always open to listening to their feelings and sharing their memories with them. This last step is just gently helping them to consciously shift their attention from what they have lost to what they still have, moving their thoughts from loss to life. This step often takes the form of encouraging them to head outside and play in the mud or climb a tree, or it might be offering to read them a favorite book or play a board game with them or maybe inviting a friend over to play.

While these three steps are in no way exhaustive, the idea behind this process is to simplify the stages of grief in a way that is accessible to parents and understandable to children. And then, when life hits hard and big losses occur such as the loss of a loved one, divorcing parents, etc. having walked through these small losses with our children sets the stage for helping them to work through the harder things while preserving a healthy parent/child connection.

Chapter 19

Chores Sh'mores

"Awww. Do I *have* to?" Who hasn't heard that response when it comes to chores? Except in this case, it's me doing the whining. No joke. The minute I hear the word 'chores,' I want to sit down or take a nap. Just the word makes me feel tired and irritable. And, since holding my children to a higher standard than I hold myself has never made sense to me, I'm certainly not going to expect cheerful compliance with a chore list, even if it comes with shiny stickers or a treasure box or an allowance. Chores are just no fun, period.

But, unless we want to live in squalor, eat off of ick-encrusted dinnerware, and wear clothes that Pepè Le Pew would find alluring, *someone* has to do *something*! With a homeschooling family of six, that 'someone' isn't going to be only me and, since my husband has repeatedly nixed my idea of taking out a second mortgage to hire a housekeeper, I have had to find a different solution to my chore aversion.

Enter, that one marketing class I took as a Literature and Written Communication major at university… "It's all in the presentation, people!"

Our family doesn't operate under a dictatorship, benevolent or otherwise, and so I needed to find a way to present our home's upkeep as a family affair, where everyone is important and needed. I also wanted to account for different ages and temperaments and unique abilities and challenges. So, I excommunicated the word 'chores' (Oh, happy day!) tossed the reward charts (more like torture charts, but we'll get to that in a minute) and cancelled the allowances. If I wanted our family to work together, I needed to act like a team member instead of like a drill sergeant.

Now, instead of people being assigned tasks, we work together on everything…

Dishes need done? My SPD (Sensory Processing Disorder) girl can't tolerate the mix of smells and textures, so she unloads the dishwasher and then scoops up the baby for some outside kitty time. My pre-med guy rinses and loads the dishwasher while my little caboose and I gather the dishes that always seem to leak out of the kitchen to the furthermost reaches of the house. In a matter of ten or fifteen chatter and clatter filled minutes, the kitchen is clean and we're off to more enjoyable pursuits.

Laundry piling up? (When isn't it, right?) Either I or one of my older children start a load and then an alternate person switches it to the dryer and starts another. Then when folding time comes, which is about once a week when the clean pile gets too big to dig through efficiently, we turn on some music and have a folding-fest. The baby rolls giggling through the clothes and tries to upend our folded piles which we rescue and 'load' onto my little caboose who pretends to be a lorry and sputters and rumbles while she delivers the clothes to the appropriate rooms.

And what about straightening? Ah, this is the best one. A couple of times a day, I trip over one too many toys and call out, "Okay, ten minute straighten!" Then I wait a moment for everybody to gather. If someone says, "Just let me finish _____, okay?" I always respect that and give them a few minutes. Just as I like them to be patient when they need me and I need to finish a phone call or some research, I model that same respect toward them. They, in turn, finish up whatever they're involved in and join me in a reasonable time (although my Renaissance Girl lives in a different time dimension depending on what book she's buried in and sometimes needs a gentle reminder). When we're all together in the offending rooms, I set my phone's timer for ten minutes, "Aaaaand…GO!" We all scurry around like crazed worker bees trying to outdo each other and, ten minutes later, the rooms are tidied and ready to be lived in once again without the danger of losing small children in the clutter.

The same scenarios play out for vacuuming, bringing in groceries, etc. The bottom line is, relationship comes before all else in our family, including housework, and in that atmosphere of respect and acceptance, we can all work together on an as-needed basis with humor and companionship. If there's any resistance, my goal is first and foremost to find out what the need is behind the behavior.

For instance, sometimes my little caboose is having a bad day and doesn't want to play lorry while we fold clothes. Since I know her unmet needs tend to be connection and attention, I share with her casually about how much everyone is needed in a family while still taking on her delivery role myself. She usually joins me, and we do it together in peace as we chat and reconnect…need met. Then, the next time, she's typically back to her sputtering, rumbling, curly-topped delivery services.

Now, about those reward/torture charts I mentioned. I tried those once many years ago, but found I just couldn't stick to it. It sounds so nice…so, well, *rewarding*, but in reality it simply rewarded my naturally organized and attentive child for being herself while punishing my little dreamer who had the best intentions, but struggled to stay on task without someone right there working alongside him. There was no defiance, no intentional irresponsibility in the unfinished tasks. There was simply a child who needed a different approach to accommodate his unique personality. Did I really want to punish a child for being who he was created to be? Could I stand there and put stickers on one sweet child's chart for simply doing what came naturally to her and watch the hurt on my other child's face, not so much because he wasn't getting a sticker, but because his little heart was broken at the thought of disappointing me? No. Just no.

So, all that said, is my house always spic-n-span? Um…NO. But is my house a happy place to be? Absolutely! I saw a sign somewhere that said, "Forgive the mess, my children are busy making memories." I loved that and thought it captured the thought well, although mine might have read something like, "Please look past the mess to the happy family in the nest!"

Chapter 20

Live What You Want Them to Learn

"What you do speaks so loud that I cannot hear what you say."
Ralph Waldo Emerson

We bring our precious little people into the world and pour our hearts and souls into lovingly raising...what?

How often do we stop and really think about what kind of a *person* we're trying to raise and what steps we're taking to accomplish that?

Character training seems to have gone out of style in some schools in favor of an all-out focus on standardized testing, but children need guidance and good examples of positive character traits if we want them to grow up to be productive members of our world. The good news is that parents who live out those positive character traits have a more powerful and lasting influence on children than any character training curriculum ever developed.

The first step, of course, is to decide just what character traits we want to model for our children. Here are a few examples of the kinds of traits we might want to focus on passing along to our children.

Generosity	*Compassion*	*Cheerfulness*
Honesty	*Friendliness*	*Self-control*
Helpfulness	*Creativity*	*Responsibility*
Resourcefulness	*Courage*	*Respect*

After considering what we want to model for our children, the next step is to look at how, or if, we're walking out those character traits in our life. Remember, our children will learn far, far more from watching what we do than from hearing what we say:

- We can lecture them eloquently about self-control, but if our children constantly see us angry and frustrated and yelling (i.e. lacking self-control), then that is what they'll internalize.

- We can preach daily sermons on honesty, but if our children see us lying to our supervisors ('cough, cough' "Sorry, I can't come in to work today. I'm sick…Okay, kids, let's go to the beach!") and cheating on our taxes, that's what they will learn.

- We can rhapsodize about the value of compassion, but if our children see us ignoring their needs in favor of our own, judging instead of helping those in need, and gossiping about others' pain, that is how they will learn to live.

The message here is this: *Consciously, intentionally, and consistently living out how we want our children to turn out is the most powerful and effective character training there is.*

Chapter 21

Is Your Child an Introvert or an Extrovert?

Gentle parenting, at its very core, is about relationship. It's about getting to know the unique individual that is our child. It's about focusing on the person, not the behavior, when challenges arise. And it's about working with, instead of against, our child as we grow together through the ages and stages of their childhood. To that end, being aware of our child's personality traits helps us to find the best ways to communicate and interact with them.

People, in general, don't fall entirely into one end of the personality spectrum or the other when it comes to being an introvert or an extrovert. Typically, they fall somewhere in the middle, with a few traits from each side, but often they do have a few more from one side or the other. It's helpful to be able to identify your child's general tendency toward introversion or extroversion, though, because therein lies the key to effectively communicating and connecting with them.

Here are a few telltale signs to help you determine whether you're raising a thinker or a doer.

Introverts:

- tend to think before they speak
- typically don't talk much
- are often uncomfortable in crowds
- tend to speak quietly and thoughtfully
- avoid the limelight
- tend to stick with an activity or conversation until it's finished
- often prefer written communication
- are often indecisive
- tend to be cautious
- tend to be shy or reserved

- often have one or two close friends
- tend to be focused, sometimes to the point of obsession
- are often serious
- tend to be thinkers

Extroverts:

- often like the limelight
- typically are comfortable in crowds
- often speak loudly and quickly
- tend to interrupt
- often have poor impulse control
- often jump from one activity to another
- tend to have trouble finishing tasks
- often think out loud
- tend to jump to conclusions
- are often decisive
- tend to be leaders
- are often easily distracted
- tend to be energetic and enthusiastic
- often are surrounded by friends
- tend to be doers

Once you have an idea what personality tendencies your child has, there are some key elements to consider when offering guidance and trying to communicate with them.

Introverts:

- often need a moment to think before responding to questions or requests
- need privacy when learning new skills
- respond more positively to guidance and praise when offered in private
- often need support when entering new situations
- tend to respond better to change when it is discussed in advance

- often need time to redirect their attention when absorbed in an activity
- don't respond well to being pushed into interacting with strangers
- often have a great need to have their personal space respected

Extroverts:

- tend to respond well when offered choices
- often need lots of physical affection and roughhousing
- respond better to independent exploration than guided teaching
- like to be complimented openly and publically
- need the freedom to try new things even when they haven't finished other things
- tend to work well in groups
- often still need time to redirect their attention when absorbed in an activity

These characteristics and suggestions aren't exhaustive, by any means, but they are springboards you can use to understand and connect with your thinkers and doers more intimately, effectively, and intentionally.

~ Gentle Parenting: Teens and Beyond ~

Chapter 22

Into the Looking Glass:
Teens and Self-Esteem

Ugly. Stupid. Fat. Worthless.

The list goes on and on and on…Teens tearing themselves apart, nitpicking their appearance, their abilities, their very worth as a human being.

Why? There are many reasons, from cruel remarks by peers to the media's photo-shopped, airbrushed portrayal of beauty to cultural, parental, and personal expectations and pressures. But one thing most teens seem to have in common as they navigate the hormonal floods and relational minefields of adolescence is an intense and often negative self-focus that magnifies the normal quirks and variations in human appearance, behavior, and capabilities to extreme proportions.

We all remember leaning close to the mirror to focus on that one seemingly *ginormous* pimple smack dab in the middle of our forehead on picture day in high school. Or maybe you will forever remember the MOST. EMBARRASSING. MOMENT. EVER. when you '*fill in the blank.*' Then, of course, there's that haircut you had in 19-'*I'll never tell.*' (**shudder**)

It's in the midst of this intense self-focus that self-image and esteem issues often begin to take root. Parents tend to respond to their teen's extreme vulnerability during this time with heart-felt reassurances such as, "Oh, Honey, you're beautiful just the way you are" and "You *are* smart. I *know* you can do this."

But, while these reassurances may be the absolute truth and may need to be said in the moment, the truth is that they may also exacerbate the issues because they point right back to where the issues are originating...*self!*

Think about it. How can *more* focus on self help solve problems that are being caused by excessive *self*-focus?

The real key to a healthy self-respect lies not in puffing self up to ever-higher levels of importance, but instead it lies in the secret magic of service. Serving others, whether by volunteering to help tutor elementary-aged students struggling with reading or feeding the homeless or spending a quiet afternoon once a week chatting with a lonely senior citizen in a nursing home, takes the focus off of self and shifts it to the needs of others.

It literally is like taking a step back from the mirror and seeing the whole picture. Without that up-close, microscopic, critical focus on the minutia, the big picture can come into focus for our teens as the little foibles and flaws common to all of us recede from monumental proportions back into their respective molehills.

In addition to a shift in focus from self to others, the gift of giving carries with it an immense blessing for our teens, as it does for all of us. When meeting someone else's need, there is a deep satisfaction and a healthy pride, a sense of purpose and meaning that gives greater context to life, and an uplifting and empowering feeling of being needed.

The return on the investment of giving is powerful and life-changing, and it is a gift we need to intentionally and regularly give to our children.

Of course, forcing anyone to serve is like leading a horse to water. In the same way you can't make a horse drink, you also can't *make* your teen serve or it isn't really serving. They won't receive the return on something they aren't investing themselves in willingly. But there are ways you can encourage your teen to serve so it is their own investment:

1. *Serve.* Modeling a giving lifestyle by letting your children see you serving others from the time they are small will have a more powerful impact than anything else you can do to encourage them to serve. Be cautious, though, about pushing aside your children's own needs in your service to others. Children who feel their needs have gone unmet in favor of others will be more likely to resent the concept of service than to embrace it. Service doesn't necessarily have to be a formal affair such as volunteering to teach Sunday School or as a regular weekly helper at your local food pantry, though if those things fit your talents and schedule they are wonderful ways of modeling service to your children. But simply seeing you helping an elderly neighbor with her lawn or stopping on the side of the road to help a stranger change a tire will have a profound influence on your children in leading them into a lifestyle that includes serving others.

2. *Let their interests lead the way.* Tapping into that stereotypical adolescent self-absorption to encourage service can give your teen a jumpstart into volunteerism. Is your teen an animal lover? Check out local animal rescue shelters for volunteer opportunities. Have a budding environmentalist? Look for local conservation areas or recycling centers and see what they have to offer. If nothing presents itself, get resourceful and help your teens create their own service opportunities.

3. *Make it a family affair.* Teens tend to be reluctant about entering new or unknown situations. Joining them will help them to overcome that first-day awkwardness they dread so much and also provide an excellent connection point to help keep your relationship strong and healthy through these sometimes turbulent years.

The bottom line here is that, instead of helping our teens to 'find themselves,' we do them a far greater service by guiding them to focus less on self and more on others. As their perspective shifts, so will their priorities, with self-absorption, self-centeredness, and selfishness evolving into open and giving hearts focused on the needs of others instead of on self. And that, the giving, the sacrifice, the laying down of self, is the true secret to a healthy self-concept.

Chapter 23

Gently Parenting Teens

Children raised with gentle parenting aren't perfect. They're children. When they're babies, they cry. When they're toddlers, they may have an occasional meltdown. As preschoolers, sometimes they whine and tattle. In middle childhood, they chatter and dream and ask endless questions on the road to discovering who they are and who they're going to be.

Gentle parenting doesn't keep children from being children, but it does help parents stay connected to their children through all of the normal ups and downs and ages and stages of childhood. It does build a foundation of trust. It does help to establish a mutually respectful relationship and a peaceful home environment. And, perhaps most importantly, it does build a strong, open communication channel.

The real 'payoff,' so to speak, comes in the teen years, though. Ask parents what causes them the most sleepless nights and, with hushed voices and wide eyes, many will tell you the very thought of adolescence, hovering like a dark shadowy terror on the horizon, makes them shudder in fear...unless they're gentle parents, that is.

Gentle parents, by and large, while they may not be entirely sure of how adolescence will play out, still feel confident that the connection, respect, and communication they've built in early childhood will carry them and their children through the teen years with their relationship intact. This confidence is well-founded. Study after study has shown that the value of a secure parent/child attachment extends beyond early childhood into adolescence.[9]

"The successful transition of adolescence is not achieved through detachment from parents. In fact, healthy transition to autonomy and adulthood is facilitated by secure attachment and emotional connectedness with parents. In a nutshell, research shows that attachment security in adolescence exerts precisely the same effect on development as it does in early childhood: a secure base fosters exploration and the development of cognitive, social and emotional competence.[10]" (Marlene M Moretti, PhD and Maya Peled, MA)

Children who enter adolescence confident in their parents' availability, compassion, and support tend to have an easier time with the transition into the greater independence, responsibility, and challenges of the teen years. The stage has been set for them to shift naturally into independence when they are ready for it because they haven't been subjected to the unnatural independence of premature, forced separation through such practices as sleep-training, self-soothing, and control-based discipline. They are often more prepared to take on responsibility because they have been a team member in the family dynamic instead of being trained to instant, unthinking obedience. And they're typically more comfortable with the idea of facing the inevitable challenges ahead because they know they won't have to face them alone.

That isn't to say that gently parented teens won't ever have any of the trials and tribulations of being adolescents. They are still human and will still have to cope with the floods of pubescent hormones and the uncertainties and pressures of looming adulthood. But having spent their earlier years of childhood being guided and equipped to face the future and being gently and consistently assured that a helping hand and listening ear are always available, they are usually well prepared to take on all that adolescence has to offer.

Chapter 24

Talking to Teens

Communication is always a huge concern for parents of adolescents. The strong, open communication channel created and mutual respect and trust foundation established in the early years through gentle parenting provide a powerful platform for a healthy parent/teen relationship. Simply put, children and teens who feel heard and understood and respected don't need to *fight* to be heard, understood, and respected. Or, conversely, they don't slip away into the sullen, angry, withdrawn teen who doesn't bother to even try to be heard anymore because they never felt heard or understood as a young child.

Again, this is not to say that the gently raised adolescent will be perfect. None of us are! But with a healthy relationship based on open, honest communication, issues can be addressed as they arise and in a respectful and timely manner instead of a teen feeling the need to go 'underground' with their behavior or problems.

So, that said, what are some practical tips for talking to teens?

1. *Honesty is paramount.* Teens will tune out faster than you can imagine if they sense you're being less than transparent with them. Only in a mutually honest environment will a teen be willing to share their deepest fears, hopes, disappointments, etc.

2. *Judgment-free zone.* Along with this goes the need to be able to say anything, anything at all, and know that they will be heard and accepted without judgment, without repercussion. Consequences for broken rules should never come as a result of a heart-to-heart discussion, or it may well be the last heart-to-heart your teen will have with you. You can and should honestly express your concern and even disappointment if

appropriate, but don't make it all about yourself or the conversation and chance for real connection will end.

3. *Respect is key.* Embarrassment is like Kryptonite to a teen. Ridiculing them, making light of their feelings, minimizing their experiences by 'one-upping' them with yours are surefire ways to shut down a conversation with a teen permanently.

4. *Reassurance is healing.* Teens need to know they are normal. They need to hear that everyone has 'bad' thoughts sometimes and that doesn't make them 'bad person.' Sharing some crazy thoughts that have popped into your head through the years and how "It's not the thought, it's what you do with the thought that matters" will help them realize they aren't abnormal. (You'd be surprised how many teens think they're abnormal! 'Normal' matters to them HUGELY.)

5. *Burn the midnight oil.* Adolescents seem to be naturally nocturnal creatures. When the house is quiet and nothing is competing for attention, guards begin to drop, emotions mellow, and in the stillness of the night, soft-voiced conversations invite deep, meaningful discussions. Don't let the busyness and business of life rob you of these sweet moments with your teens who will so very soon be off on their own in the adult world.

Chapter 25

Dealing with the Hard Stuff

Addressing difficult life issues with teens is not something most parents look forward to, particularly, and often flat out dread. Some parents just don't address these issues, period, often with excuses such as, "They need to find out what they believe for themselves."

But simply avoiding talking about difficult issues doesn't make them go away, and often teens left to fend for themselves become overwhelmed with societal pressures, an endless array of choices, and conflicting information. Leaving them to "figure out what they believe themselves" just leaves them without the guidance and wisdom they need from those they trust the most and may lead to feelings of resentment and abandonment as well as poor choices.

It can, of course, be challenging to address hard issues like sex, morality, war, politics, religion, etc. with your teen. Teenagers do a fantastic imitation of bloodhounds. Hypocrisy, fear, 'smudging' the truth, you name it, they can sniff it out in a heartbeat! When talking about these difficult life issues, it's far better to be transparent about any doubts or failings or confusion you may have because your teen will know if you try to gloss it over.

Got some skeletons in your closet? Dust them off and pull them out as object lessons and connection points. Your teen will learn more from one confession (no need to go into graphic detail) than from a hundred lectures.

Ambivalent about current events? Discuss the inner conflict you're having.

Passionate about your spiritual beliefs? Tell them how that feels and what brought you to that point.

Sharing your heart, your experiences, your struggles, honestly and often, with your teen will make an impact on them that no amount of bookwork or lecturing or training can possibly match. Keep in mind, too, that this is a life conversation and not just confined to adolescence. Beginning this kind of sharing early in your child's life in age-appropriate ways establishes the vital communication channel that is central to gentle parenting, and keeping the conversation open-ended helps to maintain healthy familial ties with your children even when they're adults, themselves. Remember, we never outgrow the human need for connection!

Chapter 26

Too Late for Teens?

So what do you do if you're the parent of a teenager and have only just discovered gentle parenting? Is it too late to implement any of the gentle parenting philosophy to establish connectedness and mutual respect and ease the transition into adulthood? And what if your teenager is in full-on rebellion mode? Is there anything gentle parenting can do for you?

The answers aren't easy, by any means. Making changes at this stage is as challenging as teens themselves can be. But, that said, there are some basic tenets that you can begin the hard work of weaving into your parenting even at this late stage:

1. *Don't engage.* Win or lose, they'll enjoy the argument, and you won't. As my grandmother always used to say, "Never wrestle with a pig. They'll love the roll in the mud whether they win or lose, and you'll just get muddy." Translated, that means that teens often simply enjoy a good debate, while adults just get frustrated.

2. *Apologize.* Take responsibility for past and present parenting mistakes. As mentioned earlier, teens can sniff out hypocrisy like bloodhounds, and acting like you're perfect (which is how they'll interpret that missing apology) smells an awful lot like hypocrisy to them.

3. *Be real.* Nothing will make a teen more resentful than you demanding behavior from them that you aren't modeling in your own life.

4. *Be available.* If you haven't been available in the past, openly let your teen know that you've made mistakes and would like to change, then let them know you are available to them, day or night, whether your favorite tv show is on or not, even if you have work to do, or emails to read, or phone calls to return...no matter what. Don't be surprised if they test you on this. Even adults tend to test out changes before we fully believe we can count on them!

5. *Communicate.* If you feel your early parenting hasn't established the open communication vital to a healthy parent/teen relationship, it isn't too late to make some renovations to bridge the gap. Just start talking...about your own life, your own struggles, your own needs, and just start sharing, about your love for them, your hopes for them, your pride in them. And start asking questions, not prying, but providing an opening for them to talk about their lives. If they aren't ready to open up yet, don't push. Just be there and ready listen when they are.

6. *Let go.* When a child reaches the teen years, it's time to begin slowly releasing them from parental controls and start letting them make more of their own choices. This is not to say that you stop being their parent, but that you begin to consciously shift your role in your teen's life further and further away from guardian and caretaker, and closer and closer to a supportive, accepting, mentoring role...in short, a friendship role that will set the stage for your relationship with your adult child. This conscious shifting on your part will help to make your teen's transition from child to adult a cooperative effort between you rather than a source of conflict.

7. *Move.* If your teen is involved with a bad group, is immersed in drugs, gangs, etc...pack up and move. I know it's easier said than done. I know there are all kinds of job and economic issues involved. I know it's a huge sacrifice. And I know they'll fight

you on it. But if everything else has failed, removing them from negative influences and situations to give them a chance at a fresh start may be the best, or only, choice. And, letting your teen know that they are the first and most important priority in your life, more important than your job, home, the life you've built, or anything else, will in and of itself go a long way toward healing your relationship. *Note: Blaming your teen for the move, inwardly or outwardly, will undermine your reasons for moving. Make peace in your own heart with the move ahead of time so you'll be up to the challenges inherent in all big life changes.*

Chapter 27

Twelve Tips for Gently Parenting Your Adult Children
(Hint: It starts when they're newborns!)

"Life is a succession of lessons which must be lived to be
understood."
Ralph Waldo Emerson

All stages of parenting come with their own unique learning
curve, their own challenges and frustrations, their own
compromises and sacrifices, and their own flubs, false steps, and
failures. From those first terror-stricken days with a newborn to
the sleep-deprived months of infancy to the challenges of
toddlerhood and beyond, parenting is a journey, not a
destination. And when subsequent little ones arrive, the journey
starts all over again as we discover that the lessons learned from
parenting one child don't always apply to the next as each have
their own incomparable personalities, quirks, and individual
identities.

The principles of gentle parenting (i.e. connection, empathy,
intentionality, respect) don't change as our children grow, just as
they don't change from one child to the next. What does change
is our understanding of those principles as we grow in wisdom
and experience as parents and human beings. The practical
application of gentle parenting principles, though, can look very
different from child to child and life stage to life stage. For
instance, with an introverted child gentle parenting might
involve a greater degree of physical proximity and emotional
support whereas with a very extroverted child it may involve a
greater degree of energy direction and respectful guidance.

This constancy of principles and individualized application of
gentle parenting is no less true when parenting our adult children
than it is when parenting our minor children. As gentle parents,

we are our children's first and best friends in the purest and truest definition of friendship. That sets the stage for the transition from the early parental years to the parent/child friendship that will characterize our relationship when our children grow into adulthood.

Gentle parenting is, in a very real sense, the intentional creation of a life-long partnership that is constantly evolving and shifting and redefining the roles of its members so that everyone's needs are met. Gently parenting adult children is simply a continuation of that partnership into the realm of adulthood.

Here are twelve practical tips to set the stage for gently parenting your children in the adult years:

1. Begin to consciously pay attention to your own parents' interactions with you. Mentally catalogue what you find helpful and what you find intrusive, what is an acceptable level of involvement, advice, and interaction and what feels overbearing or lacking. Make a mental (or actual!) note to remember those feelings when your own children become adults.

2. Remember, parenting is literally on-the-job learning. Your parents are discovering by trial and error (often lots of error) what their roles and boundaries are in this uncharted territory of parenting adults. Model giving your parents grace when they overstep or underplay their roles. This will set the stage for your children to extend the same grace to you when seemingly overnight you suddenly find yourself learning to parent your own adult children.

3. While your child is an infant, meet their needs swiftly, consistently, and gently. They won't remember what you did or didn't do at this stage, but they will always carry with them how it made them feel. Make sure what they feel is safe, secure, and loved so that is they will take with them into adulthood.

4. When your child reaches toddlerhood, focus on connection rather than correction. What will matter most in later years won't be whether they wore matching shoes or left the park without pitching a fit. What will matter is whether they felt heard, understood, and respected.

5. As your child moves into the preschool and early childhood years, focus on communication, whether that takes the form of whining, tattling, endless questions or some combination of all three. Continue to build a trust relationship by hearing their heart rather than their tone and responding with gentle guidance.

6. When your child reaches the middle stages of childhood, listening to the endless stories from your chatterbox or offering empathy and quiet support to your dreamer will help them as they explore who they are and who they want to be when they grow up. You are building the friendship of a lifetime in these interactions, so make them a priority!

7. Once your child enters the teen years, consciously begin to gradually shift your role into a supporting rather than a leading act. Listen not just to their words, their attitudes, their hormones, their angst. Listen instead to their struggles, their hopes, their dreams, their fears. Remember, you are the only adult in the relationship at this point. They still have a lot of maturing to do. Practice self-control. Be honest about your own struggles, fears, and failings. You'll be amazed at what a connection point that is as your teen discovers that they aren't alone in their humanness. Be the first one to listen, the first one to forgive, the first one to apologize, the first one to understand, the first one to back down and try to find another way when the going gets tough.

8. When your child becomes an adult, let them set the pace. Some children will hit eighteen and be ready to move into a university dorm or get a job and an apartment right away. Others will need a slower transition. They may need to stay at home while going to university or while taking some time to try out different jobs as they explore this strange new world of

adulthood. If the time comes that you feel they need a gentle nudge out of the nest, you can help them to find an acceptable roommate or two and guide them through the process of settling into independent adulthood.

9. Once your child is out on their own, your role will shift fully to a support system. Offering unsolicited advice is fine as long as it is briefly stated...*once*. After that, it becomes intrusive. Offers of help and invitations to family events, etc. should follow the same guidelines.

10. When your child starts a family of their own, consciously bring to mind how you felt at various times when your own parents supported you in your new role and/or interfered with the establishment of your new little family. Acknowledge to yourself and to them that they won't do everything the way you did, that they will make decisions you wouldn't make, that you will offer advice that won't be heeded, and that they will make mistakes and have to learn from them just like you did.

11. On the subject of making mistakes, remember, just as you wouldn't want every youthful mistake, every wrong choice, every unfortunate decision to be broadcast to the world or even just joked about privately instead of being left in the past where it belongs, be sure to practice 'The Golden Rule of Parenting' and treat your children how you like to be treated.

12. Keep in mind that the person you are now isn't the person you were when you first started out on your journey into adulthood. Expecting your young adult children to think and experience and process life and events the way that you do now is like expecting a newborn baby to be able to pick up a book and read it.

~ Conclusion: Setting Yourself Up For Success ~

Chapter 28

Twelve Steps to Gentle Parenting

It's been said that it takes twenty-one days to make or break a habit and that change comes easiest and lasts longest when it's undertaken in small, bite-sized chunks. Those same principles apply when trying to transform your parenting, as well. Simply resolving on January 1st that, from that day forward, you are going to be a gentle parent and trying to change everything all at once is just setting yourself up for disappointment, frustration, and, more than likely, failure, followed by that age-old enemy of peace…mommy guilt.

Instead, try setting yourself up for success by taking a year of 'baby steps' to create real, lasting transformation in your parenting. Here are twelve steps you can start any time of the year, not just on January 1st, that offer practical, effective guidance to help you on your journey to gentle parenting. Keep in mind, though, that failure is a natural, normal part of change, so remember to give yourself grace when you fail. (Also, giving yourself grace is good practice for learning to extend that same grace to your children, which is a hallmark of gentle parenting!)

January (Step 1)

Slow down! ~ Gentle parenting is, at its core, based on a strong, healthy parent/child connection, so intentionally including time in your life to build and maintain that connection is vital. Start the year off by examining your daily and weekly schedule and looking for things to reduce or eliminate. Add up how much time your children spend in school, sleeping, in daycare, with babysitters, at sports practices, in music lessons, etc. and look at how much or little time is left over. Time for your family to connect, time to play, time to simply be, are just as important as those other activities, if not more so! Eliminate and reduce what you can, and look for ways to build connection into the things you can't eliminate. For instance, if your child has homework each night, why not sit down and work through the homework with them? As humans, we learn better through interaction, anyway, so you'll not only be connecting, you'll be enriching your child's education in the process! Another area that might benefit from a connection 'rehab' is that morning rush to get ready and out the door. Try getting everyone up a half hour earlier to ease the morning stresses that often lead to conflict and can result in a parent/child disconnect.

February (Step 2)

Listen! ~ Once you've slowed down enough to breathe, it's time to stretch yourself and grow as a parent. Like most changes in life, it won't come easy, but the rewards are well worth it. Fred Rogers said, "Listening is where love begins," meaning that when we listen, we really get to know someone, learn about what motivates them, and understand their thoughts, hopes, dreams, hurts, disappointments, etc. All behaviors communicate underlying needs, and what we learn about the inner life of our children by listening to them will help us to focus on the needs behind the behaviors instead of simply correcting the 'symptoms' (i.e. the behavior).

As a parent, it may seem instinctive to insist that our children listen to us so that our guidance and/or correction can be heard. In fact, the number one complaint I get from most parents is, "My children just don't listen!" to which I respond, "Do you?"

The reality is that if a child doesn't feel they are being heard, then even if they stand silently 'listening' while we lecture or rant or even just talk, the child is simply rehearsing in their brain what they want to say rather than actually doing any effective listening. As the only adults in the parent/child relationship, it's up to the parent to be the first to listen, to *really* listen, because we are the ones with the maturity and self-control to be able to patiently wait to be heard.

March (Step 3)

Live what you want them to learn! ~ Ralph Waldo Emerson said, "What you do speaks so loud that I cannot hear what you say." Consciously, intentionally, and consistently living out how you want your children to turn out is the most powerful and effective character training there is. If you want your children to be kind, be kind. If you want them to be respectful, respect them. If you want them to learn self-control, model self-control. If you want them to be compassionate, treat them with compassion. If you want them to feel joy, enjoy them. If you want them to feel valuable, treasure them. The bottom line is, your children are always watching and learning, so make sure what they see in you is what you want to see in them!

April (Step 4)

Breathe! ~ We all get overwhelmed by the seemingly endless demands of life at times, so this month remind yourself to relax and consciously focus on enjoying your children. It's just a fact of human nature that when we enjoy something, we pay more attention to it, value it, and treat it better. Applying that fact to parenting, it makes sense to be intentional about taking time to laugh and hug and simply be with our children. Check out the 'bucket list' in chapter 15 full of ideas for simple, memorable fun to share with life's most precious treasures, your children!

May (Step 5)

Book it! ~ It's been said that our treasure lies where our time, attention, and love is invested. While having special family outings and activities is a wonderful way to enjoy our children, it is in the daily routines and busyness of life that the parent/child connection can often suffer the most. One of the best ways to stay connected with our children is to build time into each day to invest in them, and one of the best investments is in a love of reading. A love of reading is born on the lap of a parent, in the soothing cadence of a mother's voice reading the same beloved story night after night, in the rhythmic sway of a rocking chair, and in the comfortable rustle of well-worn pages being turned one after another after another. A quiet bedtime routine that includes a nighttime story will not only help bedtime to be happier and smoother, but will also incorporate vital time for you to reconnect with your children at the end of every day.

June (Step 6)

Turn your 'no's' into 'yes's'! ~ In any home, like in any civilized society, boundaries are necessary for everyone's safety and comfort. With gentle parenting, setting limits focuses on connection and empathetic communication rather than control and punitive consequences. This month try setting limits using gentle parenting by turning your 'no's' into 'yes's.' Instead of "No, you can't have ice cream until after dinner," try "I know you love ice cream. I do, too! We're getting ready to eat right now, but what flavor would you like after dinner?" This invites cooperation instead of triggering opposition, another hallmark of gentle parenting.

July (Step 7)

Play! ~ They say that the family that plays together, stays together, and there's great truth to that. Play is the language of childhood, and through play we get to know and connect with our children on their turf, in their native language, and on their terms. It's a powerful moment in a parent's life when they suddenly see their sweet little one as a separate, intelligent, worthy human being who can plan, make decisions, snap out orders, and lead other humans on a journey through an imaginary rainforest or on a trip through outer space. This month, try taking on the role of follower in your child's land of make-believe, and you'll discover a whole new world in which your child is strong, confident, and capable, and you'll come away with a deeper connection with and appreciation for the *person*, not just the child.

August (Step 8)

Eat well! ~ Along with all of the exercise you'll be getting playing with your child, take stock of the kinds of food you're providing to fuel their little engines and enrich their minds. Good nutrition may not be the first thought that pops into people's minds when they think of gentle parenting, but studies have shown that many behavior issues and sleep problems have their root in unhealthy eating habits, nutrient-poor diets, and food additives (dyes, preservatives, etc.). Children, especially littler ones, don't take change well as a general rule, and changes to the foods they eat are on top of the list of changes they'll resist. As a gentle parent, working with, instead of against, our children will help to make eating healthy a fun family project instead of a food fight. Try letting your children help you make weekly menus and shop for the fresh ingredients you'll be using, and let them help you cook, too. If they feel like they are a part of the change instead of a victim of it, they're far more likely to cooperate. If you have picky eaters, don't hesitate to serve them the same foods you normally do, just with a few added healthy ingredients slipped in to make them healthier. For ideas on ways to make healthy changes more fun, turn back to chapter 9.

September (Step 9)

Don't forget your funny bone! ~ Often the best parenting advice is simply, "Chill out! Relax! Laugh a little, for goodness' sake!" Sometimes as parents we get so caught up in 'fixing' our children that all we see are problems. We start focusing so much on preparing our children for their future that we forget to let them live in the present. One of the main problems with that is that children are, by their very nature, creatures of the 'now,' living fully immersed in each present moment. This month, pull out your dusty, old funny-bone, the one that used to keep you in stitches when you were a child, and laugh, on purpose, every day with your child. You'll be amazed at how a good belly laugh can turn even the worst day into something a little easier to handle and how much a giggle-fest can heal the little rifts that tend to occur in the parent/child connection throughout each day.

October (Step 10)

If you build it, they will come! ~ A shared project can offer a real chance to get to know your child on an entirely new level, so this month find something to build together. Choose something they are interested in, whether it's a model rocket or tree fort, and watch them blossom as they learn and build and grow. Your role is supportive--finding the materials, helping to read the instructions, offering suggestions or help when they struggle, etc. Simply being there through the process will enrich your connection with your child and offer you valuable insights into their interests and learning style, which will provide tools for you to use when helping them with their homework or homeschooling them.

November (Step 11)

Gratitude is an attitude! ~ Teaching our children to be grateful involves far more than simply instructing them to say, "Thank you." We all want to be appreciated, and children are no different. Remember, modeling the things we want to see in our children is the single most powerful mode of instruction, so living a life of gratitude ourselves goes a long way toward raising our little ones to be happy, grateful humans. Openly appreciating our children, telling them what we like about them, and thanking them for the things they do is a sure-fire way of inspiring an attitude of gratitude in their little hearts. This month, be intentional in finding things to praise in your children. Don't be falsely enthusiastic or use "Good job!" as a brush-off to get them to leave you alone. Instead, honestly tell them what you like about them. Tell them 'thank you' when they remember to brush their teeth without being told or help their little sister with her block tower. Let them know you think their artwork is beautiful and don't hesitate to give them a pat on the back for a job well done when they straighten their room. Remember, it is the hungry child, not the satisfied child, who craves food, and, in the same way, it is *unmet* needs that lead to attention seeking behaviors and *unspoken* approval that can create 'praise junkies' as the unpraised child seeks to fill the very human need we all have for validation.

December (Step 12)

Celebrate! ~ Take time this month to give yourself a pat on the back for working toward your goal of becoming a gentle parent. Congratulate yourself for all that you've accomplished and take stock of your successes as well as your failures. Don't focus on your mistakes. Simply learn from them, forgive yourself, and move forward. Look back at where you were as a parent a year ago and compare that to where you are now. Don't worry if you haven't come as far as you'd like. Remember to give yourself grace. Life is for living and learning and growing, and another year is about to start with a chance to move forward into a new beginning. Everything you've invested in your children in the last year has been worthwhile, and everything you'll invest in the coming years will build on the foundation you've begun. So take this month to celebrate *you* and to enjoy the return on your investment!

~~~~~~~~

Do you see a theme throughout this gentle parenting '12-step program'? Getting to know and enjoy your children as individuals, intentionally focusing on building and maintaining a strong and healthy parent/child connection, and living what you want your children to learn are the bedrocks of gentle parenting. Walking through these steps, revisiting them when you find yourself struggling, and appreciating the incredible, miraculous gifts that each individual child brings into the world will keep you growing as a gentle parent day after day, month after month, year after year.

Live. Laugh. Love. Enjoy!

References

1. McKenna, Dr. James J.. "Mother-Baby Behavioral Sleep Laboratory." *University of Notre Dame, College of Arts and Letters*. N.p., n.d. Web. 6 Feb 2013. <http://cosleeping.nd.edu/safe-co-sleeping-guidelines/>.

2. Schore, A.N. (2000). Attachment and the regulation of the right brain. *Attachment & Human Development*, 2, 23-47.

3. Sears, Dr. William. *SIDS: A Parent's Guide to Understanding and Preventing Sudden Infant Death Syndrome* . Little Brown & Co, 1995. Print. <http://www.amazon.com/SIDS-Parents-Understanding-Preventing-Syndrome/dp/0316779121/ref=sr_1_1?s=books&ie=UTF8&qid=1360194660&sr=1-1&keywords=0316779121>.

4. Daly, Steven and Peter Hartmann. "Infant Demand and Milk Supply. Part 1: Infant Demand and Milk Production in Lactating Women." *Journal of Human Lactation I* I(l) 1995; p. 21-26.

5. Melissa Bartick, MD, MSca, Arnold Reinhold, MBA, . "The Burden of Suboptimal Breastfeeding in the United States: A Pediatric Cost Analysis." *Journal of the American Academy of Pediatrics* . (2010): n. page. Web. 6 Feb. 2013. <http://pediatrics.aappublications.org/content/early/2010/04/05/peds.2009-1616.abstract>.

6. Falco, Miriam. "New advice to prevent and correct flat head syndrome in babies." *CNN Health*. 28 Nov 2011: n. page. Web. 7 Feb. 2013. <http://thechart.blogs.cnn.com/2011/11/28/new-advice-to-prevent-and-correct-flat-head-syndrome-in-babies/>.

7. Medical Advisory Board, . "IHDI Educational Statement." *International Hip Dysplasia Institute*. 2012: n. page. Web. 7 Feb. 2013. <http://www.hipdysplasia.org/Developmental-Dysplasia-Of-The-Hip/Prevention/Baby-Carriers-Seats-and-Other-Equipment/>.

8. Walters, Barbara, perf. *Barbara Walters interviews Sean Connery on slapping women*. Perf. Sean Connery. 1987. Web. 7 Feb 2013. <http://www.youtube.com/watch?feature=player_embedded&v=3FgMLROTqJ0>.

9.   Neufeld, Ph.D., Gordon. *Hold On to Your Kids: Why Parents Need to Matter More Than Peers* . Ballantine Books, 2006. Print. <http://www.amazon.com/Hold-Your-Kids-Parents-Matter/dp/0375760288

10.   Marlene M Moretti, PhD and Maya Peled, MA, . "Adolescent-parent attachment: Bonds that support healthy development." *US National Library of Medicine.* 9. (2004): 551-555. Web. 6 Feb. 2013. <http://www.ncbi.nlm.nih.gov/pmc/articles/PMC2724162/ >.

11.   Onya Baby, . "Can babywearing eliminate the need for tummy time?." N.p., 04 02 2012. Web. Web. 15 Feb. 2013. <http://onyababy.com/blog/2012/02/can-babywearing-eliminate-the-need-for-tummy-time/>.

6138547R00063

Made in the USA
San Bernardino, CA
05 December 2013